LITERARY
SHORTS
ANTHOLOGY

ACKNOWLEDGEMENTS

Written and edited by Andrew McCallum and Kate Oliver

Published by the English and Media Centre, 18 Compton Terrace, London, N1 2UN

© 2014

ISBN: 978 1 906101 32 9

Printed by: Stephens and George Ltd

Cover: Andy Bridge/Alamy

Thanks to Matt McHugh for trialling and commenting on draft material, to Barbara Bleiman and Lucy Webster for advice and editing, to Stephen Donovan, Pam Dix and Sue Adler for advice on selecting short stories, and to teachers attending KS3 courses at the English and Media Centre in 2013-14.

Thanks to the following writers, publishers, agents and estates for giving permission to reproduce copyrighted material:

Paz Literary Agency for 'Two Words' in Isabel Allende, *The Stories of Eva Luna* Penguin Books 1991 and 'One of These Days' in Gabriel Garcia Marquez in *No-One Writes to the Colonel*; English Translation © 1968 by Harper and Row, Publishers Inc New York; Houghton Mifflin Harcourt for 'The Third-Floor Bedroom' © 2011 Kate DiCamillo in *The Chronicles of Harris Burdick* first published in USA 2011 by Houghton Mifflin Harcourt Publishing Ltd Illustration © 1984 Chris Van Allsburg; Jamila Gavin, 'Paradise Carpet' from *Out of the Shadow* (1 Nov 2002) reproduced by permission of Egmont Books, London; The Marsh Agency for Yasar Kemal 'The White Trousers' © 1968 Yasar Kemal in *Anatolian Tales* Published by Writers and Readers Publishing Cooperative Society Ltd 1983 © 1968 in English translation by William Collins and Sons & Co Ltd London; Joe R. Lansdale & Baror International, Inc. for 'Dog, Cat, and Baby', by Joe R. Lansdale; David Higham for G. McCaughrean: 'The Gulf' © Geraldine McCaughrean 1999 published in *Dare to be Different*: a celebration of freedom in association with Amnesty International Bloomsbury Children's Books, 'The Flowers', in Alice Walker, *The Complete Stories* Phoenix Paperbacks (2005) and 'The Hitch-hiker', in Roald Dahl, *The Complete Short Stories Vol. 2* Penguin Books (2013); Felicity Bryan Agency and Meg Rosoff © 2006 Meg Rosoff for 'Resigned' first published in *Shining On A Collection of Stories in Aid of the Teen Cancer Trust* (Delacourte Press, an imprint of Random House Children's Books, a division of Random House Inc New York; Penguin for Updike, John, 'Oliver's Evolution' from *Licks of Love Short Stories and Sequel*, (Hamish Hamilton, 2000) copyright © John Updike, 2000; Press Association for 'Very Short Short Stories' published in *The Guardian* March 2007; The Marsh Agency for Ngugi wa Thiong'o 'The Return'; Jean Rhys 'I Used to Live Here': the rights are held by Jean Rhys Ltd, and all copying in whatever format is prohibited without prior written consent of the copyright holder; Copyright © William Trevor, 'Mrs Silly' from William Trevor: *Collected Stories (Volume I)*, Viking Press, Penguin Group, 2009. Reproduced with the kind permission of Johnson & Alcock Ltd.

Literary Shorts – An Anthology © English & Media Centre, 2014

CONTENTS

	Introduction	4
1.	The Diamond Necklace, by Guy de Maupassant (1884)	5
2.	A Matter of Fact, by Rudyard Kipling (1892)	15
3.	Subha, by Rabindranath Tagore (1898)	25
4.	The Open Window, by Saki (1914)	31
5.	A Cup of Tea, by Katherine Mansfield (1922)	35
6.	Old Mrs Chundle, by Thomas Hardy (1929)	44
7.	One of these Days, by Gabriel Garcia Marquez (1962)	54
8.	The Return, by Ngugi Wa Thiong'o (1965)	58
9.	The White Trousers, by Yaşar Kemal (1968)	64
10.	The Flowers, by Alice Walker (1973)	73
11.	Mrs Silly, by William Trevor (1975)	75
12.	I Used to Live Here Once, by Jean Rhys (1976)	96
13.	The Hitch-hiker, by Roald Dahl (1977)	98
14.	Two Words, by Isabel Allende (1989)	112
15.	Oliver's Evolution, by John Updike (1998)	120
16.	Dog, Cat, and Baby, by Joe R. Lansdale (1999)	122
17.	The Gulf, by Geraldine McCaughrean (1999)	125
18.	The Paradise Carpet, by Jamila Gavin (2002)	129
19.	Resigned, by Meg Rosoff (2011)	134
20.	Happily Ever After, by Barbara Bleiman (2011)	144
21.	The Third-floor Bedroom, by Kate DiCamillo (2011)	153

INTRODUCTION

Welcome to *Literary Shorts*, an anthology of short stories to challenge, entertain and inspire.

The stories have been carefully selected to offer you a wide range of rich reading experiences. With texts from the 19th, 20th and 21st centuries, by authors from all six continents, you're sure to find plenty to enjoy.

The selection is designed to offer you multiple opportunities to develop your critical, creative and comparative skills. Hence the title of the anthology's accompanying resource pack – *Literary Shorts: Critical, Creative and Comparative Approaches for KS3*. Not only does this contain material to go with each story, but it also offers exciting ways to explore key features of literary texts, such as setting, structure and character. These can be adapted to go with the stories you most want to read and are a fantastic way to develop the analytical skills so crucial to English study as you grow older.

You'll love the stories in this anthology and you'll love what the accompanying resources allow you to do with them.

THE DIAMOND NECKLACE

GUY DE MAUPASSANT

> **Guy de Maupassant** (1850-1893) was an influential French writer, considered to be one of the godfathers of the modern short story. His work belongs to the 'realist' school of literature, which attempts to show the details of everyday life as closely as possible in writing.
>
> 'The Diamond Necklace', first published in 1884, is one of his most liked short stories and is well known for its ending.

She was one of those pretty, charming girls who are sometimes born, as if by an accident of fate, into a family of ordinary workers. She had no dowry, no aspirations, no way of becoming well-known, or understood, or loved, or married to a rich and distinguished man, and so she allowed herself to be married off to a lowly pen pusher from the Ministry of Education.

She had simple tastes, since she couldn't afford any better, and yet she was as miserable as if she had once been a member of the upper classes. For women can get past caste or class, using beauty, grace and charm to get on instead of high birth and a good family. The only way to rank women is by their natural refinement, their instinct for elegance, their quick thinking, and these qualities can make an ordinary woman the equal of the finest lady.

She suffered endlessly, feeling herself to have been born for a life of delicacy and luxury. She hated the poverty of her lodgings, the bare walls, the worn chairs, the ugly curtains. All these things, which another woman of her class would not even notice, tormented her and made her resentful. The sight of the little Breton girl who did their modest housework brought on bitter disappointment and hopeless dreams. She imagined silent antechambers, lined with Oriental tapestries, lit by bronze candelabras, with two imposing footmen in knee breeches dozing in huge armchairs, overcome by the heavy warmth of the stove. She imagined vast reception rooms hung with antique silks, fine pieces of furniture laden with priceless ornaments, and intimate, perfumed reception rooms made for late afternoon conversations with the closest of friends – famous, sought after men, the ones all women desire and crave the attentions of.

When she sat down to dinner opposite her husband, at a round table covered with the same tablecloth they had used for three days in a row, and he lifted the lid from the pot exclaiming delightedly: 'Stew! Nothing could be better than that!' she imagined fine meals, gleaming silver cutlery, tapestries on the walls depicting people from times past and strange birds flying in a magical forest. She imagined exquisite dishes, served on beautiful china. She imagined herself receiving whispered gallantries with a sphinx-like smile, while eating the pink flesh of a trout or the wing of a grouse.

She had no fine clothes, no jewels, nothing like that. And yet these were the only things she loved; she was made for them, she felt. She so longed to please, to be envied, to be desired and sought after.

She had a rich friend, an old schoolmate from the convent, whom she no longer wanted to visit because it made her so sad when she returned home. She would cry for whole days with heartache and regret, in despair and misery.

***

Then, one evening, her husband came back from work looking pleased with himself and holding a large envelope in his hand. 'Here you are,' he said. 'Something for you.'

She quickly tore into the paper and pulled out a card, which bore these words:

> The Minister of Education and Madame Georges Ramponneau request the honour of the company of Monsieur and Madame Loisel at the Ministry on the evening of Monday 18th January.

Instead of being delighted, as her husband had hoped, she threw the invitation onto the table resentfully, muttering:

'What do you want me to do with that?'

'But sweetheart, I thought you'd be pleased. You never go out, and this is a wonderful opportunity. I went to a lot of trouble to get this invitation. Everyone wants one; it's a very select gathering and they aren't giving out many invitations to ordinary clerks like me. You'll get to see all the most important people.'

Giving him an angry look, she exclaimed impatiently:

'And what do you think I could possibly wear to this event?'

He had not thought of that. He stammered:

'Well, the gown you wear to the theatre. That seems very nice, to me…'

He stopped, confused and at a loss, noticing that his wife was crying. Two huge tears rolled slowly from the corners of her eyes towards the corners of her mouth. He asked:

'What's the matter? What's the matter?'

With a tremendous effort, she got her emotions under control and, wiping away her tears, answered him in a calm voice:

'Nothing. It's just that I don't have anything to wear and so I can't go to the party. Give the invitation to a colleague whose wife can be better dressed than me.'

He was in despair. He tried again:

'Let's see, Mathilde. What would it cost? A decent dress, one you could use for other things afterwards. Something very simple.'

She thought for several seconds, working out how much she would need, but also calculating how much she could ask for without getting an immediate refusal and an exclamation of horror from the clerk, who was careful with his money.

Eventually she replied, hesitantly:

'I'm not sure exactly, but I think I could manage to find something for four hundred francs.'

His face grew a little pale because that was exactly the amount he was setting aside to treat himself to a gun so that he could join a shooting party next summer on the Nanterre plain, with a group of friends who went there on Sundays to shoot larks.

'Very well,' he said. 'Four hundred francs it is. Just try to get a really beautiful dress.'

***

The day of the ball drew near and Madame Loisel seemed sad, uneasy, anxious, even though her dress was ready. One evening, her husband said to her:

'What's the matter with you? You haven't been yourself for the last three days.'

And she replied:

'What's bothering me is that I don't have any jewellery to wear, not a single stone. I'll look as poor as I always do. I'd almost rather not go to the party at all.'

'You could wear fresh flowers,' said her husband. 'They're very stylish at this time of year. You can get two or three beautiful roses for ten francs.'

She was not at all convinced.

'No…There's nothing more humiliating than looking poor when you're surrounded by rich women.'

But her husband cried:

'You silly thing! Go and see your friend, Madame Forestier, and ask her to lend you some jewels. You're close enough to her to do that.'

She uttered a cry of joy:

'That's true! I never thought of that!'

The next day, she went to see her friend and explained the problem. Mme Forestier went to her mirrored wardrobe, took out a large jewellery box, brought it to Mme Loisel, opened it and said:

'Choose something, dear.'

First she saw bracelets, then a pearl necklace, then an exquisitely made gold Venetian cross studded with gems. She tried on each piece in the mirror, hesitating, not wanting to part with any of them, to give them back. She kept asking:

'Do you have anything else?'

'Of course. Have a look. I don't know what kind of thing you like.'

Suddenly she discovered, in a black satin box, a beautiful string of diamonds; her heart began to beat with an uncontrollable desire. Her hands trembled as she picked it up. She put it on, over her high-necked dress, and was lost in ecstasy at her own reflection.

Then she asked hesitantly, anxiously:

'Would you lend me this? Just this?'

'Of course. Definitely.'

She threw her arms around her friend's neck, gave her a big kiss, and fled with her treasure.

The day of the party arrived. Mme Loisel was a success. She was the prettiest of them all, elegant, gracious, smiling and wildly happy. All the men looked at her, asked her name, wanted to be introduced to her. All the secretaries of state wanted to waltz with her. The Minister noticed her.

She danced as if intoxicated, wildly, drunk with pleasure, forgetting everything except the triumph of her beauty, the glory of her success, in a sort of cloud of happiness created by all the tributes paid to her, all the admiration, by the desire she had aroused, by the complete victory which was so sweet to her woman's heart.

She left at about four o' clock in the morning. Her husband had been asleep since midnight in a deserted little room with three other men whose wives were really enjoying themselves.

Over her shoulders he threw the coat he had brought for her to go home in, the modest clothing of her normal life, and the poverty of it contrasted with the elegance of the ball gown. She felt the contrast and wanted to get away, before it could be noticed by the other women, who were wrapping themselves in costly furs.

Loisel held her back:

'Wait a bit. You'll catch cold out there. I'll go and call a cab.'

But she didn't listen to him and rushed down the stairs. When they reached the street, they couldn't find a cab; they began searching for one, shouting after drivers they saw going past in the distance.

They went down towards the Seine, desperate and shivering. At last, on the dock, they found one of those ancient, nightprowling cabs that you only see in Paris after dark, as if they were ashamed to show their shabbiness during the day.

It took them to their door on Rue des Martyrs and they walked sadly up to their flat. It was all over for her. And he, meanwhile, was thinking about the fact that he had to be at the office by ten.

She took off the old coat that covered her shoulders in front of the mirror, so as to see herself one more time in her full glory. But she let out a sudden cry. The necklace was no longer around her neck!

Her husband, who was already half undressed, asked:

'What's the matter with you?'

She turned towards him in a panic:

'I... I... I don't have Mme Forestier's necklace anymore.'

He stood up, bewildered:

'What? How? That's not possible!'

And they searched in the folds of her dress, in the folds of her coat, in the pockets, everywhere. It was not to be found.

He asked:

'Are you sure you still had it when we left the ball?'

'Yes, I touched it in the hall at the Ministry.'

'But if you'd lost it in the street, we would have heard it fall. It must be in the cab.'

'Yes, that seems likely. Did you take the cab's number?'

'No. How about you? Did you notice it?'

'No.'

They looked at each other, horrified. Eventually, Loisel got dressed again.

'I'll go,' he said. 'I'll retrace our steps and see if I can find it.'

And he went out. She stayed in her evening gown, without the strength to take herself to bed, collapsed on a chair, no fire, unable to think.

Her husband came back seven hours later. He had found nothing.

He went to the police station, to the newspapers to offer a reward, to the cab companies, in fact anywhere that seemed to him to offer the tiniest ray of hope.

She waited all day, in the same state of bewilderment at this terrible disaster.

Loisel, his face hollow and pale, returned that evening having found nothing.

'You must,' he said, 'write to your friend and say that you've broken the clasp and we're getting it repaired. That will buy us some time.'

She wrote what he dictated.

***

By the end of the week, they had completely lost hope.

And Loisel, who had aged five years, declared:

'We must find a way to replace the necklace.'

The next day, they took the box that had held the necklace, and went to the jeweller's whose name was inside. He looked in his books:

'It wasn't me who sold this necklace madame, I only supplied the clasp.'

So they went from jeweller to jeweller, searching for an identical necklace, trying to remember it accurately, both of them sick with worry and grief.

They found a diamond necklace which seemed to them to be exactly the same as the one they had lost in a shop at Palais Royal. It was priced at forty thousand francs. They could have it for thirty-six thousand.

They begged the jeweller not to sell it to anyone for three days. And they made a deal with him that he would buy this one back from them for thirty-four thousand, if they found the one they had lost before the end of February.

Loisel had eighteen thousand francs left to him by his father. He would have to borrow the rest.

So he borrowed, asking for a thousand francs from one person, five hundred from another, five Louis here, three Louis there. He signed promissory notes, entered into ruinous agreements, did business with usurers and every kind of lender. He mortgaged the rest of his life, risked his signature without any idea whether he would be able to repay, and, afraid of the trouble that lay ahead, of the black misery he was bringing down upon himself, of the prospect of physical deprivation and moral torment, he went to get the new string of diamonds, and to place thirty-six thousand francs on the jeweller's counter.

When Mme Loisel returned the necklace, Mme Forestier said, in a rather resentful way:

'You really should've given it back to me sooner. I might have needed it.'

She didn't open the box, something her friend had worried about. If she'd noticed that it was a replacement, what would she have thought? What would she have said? Would she have taken her for a thief?

***

Madame Loisel came to know the hard life of the needy. Unexpectedly, however, she made up her mind to play her part heroically. The terrible debt had to be paid. And pay it she would. They dismissed the maid, changed lodgings, rented an attic room.

She came to know what it meant to do heavy housework and hateful kitchen jobs. She washed up, wearing out her pink nails scrubbing the greasy crockery and the bottoms of pans. She did the dirty laundry, the shirts and the dishcloths and dried them on the line; she took the rubbish down to the street every morning and brought up the water, stopping on each landing to catch her breath. And, dressed as the poor woman she now was, she went to the fruit shop, the butcher, the grocer, a basket on her arm, haggling, insulted, hanging onto every wretched penny.

Each month they paid off some debts and renewed others to give them more time.

The husband worked in the evenings, keeping the accounts for a shopkeeper and often, at night, he did copy work for five pennies a page.

And this life lasted for ten years.

At the end of ten years, everything was paid off, everything, including the usurer's charges and the accumulated interest.

Mme Loisel seemed to have aged, now. She had become one of those tough and hard and coarse women who come from a poor household. Her hair was badly styled, her skirts awry, her hands reddened, she talked loudly, sloshing the water over the floorboards as she washed them. But every now and then, when her husband was at the office, she sat by the window and she day-dreamed about that evening long ago, and the ball where she had been so beautiful and so much admired.

What might have happened if she had never lost the necklace? Who knows? Who knows? How strange life is, how unpredictable! How little it takes to ruin you, or to save you!

***

Then one Sunday she was taking a walk along the Champs-Elysee to relax after a week of hard work, when she suddenly caught sight of a woman who was walking with a child. It was Mme Forestier, still young, still beautiful, still attractive.

Mme Loisel felt emotional. Should she speak to her? Yes, of course she should. And now that everything was paid off, she could tell her all about it. Why not?

She went nearer.

'Hello, Jeanne.'

Her friend did not recognise her and was surprised at being spoken to in such a familiar way by this lower class woman. She stammered:

'But... madame! I don't know... you must be mistaken.'

'No. I'm Mathilde Loisel.'

Her friend gave a cry.

'Oh!... Poor Mathilde, you've changed so much!'

'Yes, I've had some hard times since I last saw you; and more than my share of trouble... and all because of you!'

'Because of me... How come?'

'You remember that beautiful string of diamonds you lent me for the Ministry ball?'

'Yes. And?'

'And, I lost it.'

'What! But you gave it back to me.'

'I gave you another one exactly like it. And we've been paying for it for the last ten years. You have to understand that it hasn't been easy, we had nothing you know... But it's finally over, I'm very glad to say.'

Mme Forestier had stopped.

'You're saying that you bought a string of diamonds to replace mine?'

'Yes. You've never noticed? They were very similar.'

And she smiled with a happiness that was proud and innocent.

Mme Forestier, deeply moved, took her by both hands.

'Oh! My poor Mathilde! Mine was fake. It was worth five hundred francs at the most!...'

A MATTER OF FACT

RUDYARD KIPLING

> **Rudyard Kipling** (1865-1936) was, in the late 19th and early 20th centuries, one of the most widely read writers in the English language. Today he remains well known for his *Just So Stories* and *The Jungle Book*, made into a much-loved animated film by Disney. His poem 'If' was voted the British public's favourite in a nationwide BBC poll.
>
> 'A Matter of Fact', first published in 1892, is a typical Kipling story, packed with adventure and mystery.
>
> This is an abridged version of the story.

There were three of us, all newspaper men, the only passengers on a little tramp steamer called the *Rathmines* that ran where her owners told her to go. There was Keller, of an American paper, on his way back to the States from palace executions in Madagascar; there was a burly half-Dutchman, called Zuyland, who owned and edited a paper up country near Johannesburg; and there was myself, who had solemnly put away all journalism.

Three ordinary men would have quarrelled through sheer boredom before they reached Southampton. We, by virtue of our craft, were anything but ordinary men. A large percentage of the tales of the world, the thirty-nine that cannot be told to ladies and the one that can, are common property coming of a common stock. We told them all, as a matter of form, with all their local and specific variants which are surprising. Then came, in the intervals of steady card-play, more personal histories of adventure and things seen and suffered: fires, and faces that opened and shut their mouths horribly at red-hot window frames; wrecks in frost and snow, reported from the sleet-sheathed rescue-tug at the risk of frostbite; long rides after diamond thieves; skirmishes on the veldt and in municipal committees with the Boers; glimpses of lazy tangled Cape politics and the mule-rule in the Transvaal; card-tales, horse-tales, woman-tales, by the score and the half hundred; till the first mate, who had seen more than us all put together, but lacked words to clothe his tales with, sat open-mouthed far into the dawn. ∥

***

In the morning of one specially warm night we three were sitting immediately in front of the wheel-house, where an old Swedish boatswain whom we called 'Frithiof the Dane' was at the wheel, pretending that he could not hear our stories. Once or twice Frithiof spun the spokes curiously, and Keller lifted his head from a long chair to ask, 'What is it? Can't you get any steerage-way on her?'

Nobody seems to know the laws that govern the pulse of the big waters. Sometimes even a landsman can tell that the solid ocean is atilt, and that the ship is working herself up a long unseen slope.

The sea was as smooth as a duck-pond, except for a regular oily swell. As I looked over the side to see where it might be following us from, the sun rose in a perfectly clear sky and struck the water with its light so sharply that it seemed as though the sea should clang like a burnished gong. The wake of the screw and the little white streak cut by the log-line hanging over the stern were the only marks on the water as far as eye could reach.

Keller rolled out of his chair and went aft to get a pineapple from the ripening stock that was hung inside the after awning.

'Frithiof, the log-line has got tired of swimming. It's coming home,' he drawled.

'What?' said Frithiof, his voice jumping several octaves.

'Coming home,' Keller repeated, leaning over the stern. I ran to his side and saw the log-line, which till then had been drawn tense over the stern railing, slacken, loop, and come up off the port quarter. Frithiof called up the speaking-tube to the bridge, and the bridge answered, 'Yes, nine knots.' Then Frithiof spoke again, and the answer was, 'What do you want of the skipper?' and Frithiof bellowed, 'Call him up.'

By this time Zuyland, Keller, and myself had caught something of Frithiof's excitement, for any emotion on shipboard is most contagious. The captain ran out of his cabin, spoke to Frithiof, looked at the log-line, jumped on the bridge, and in a minute we felt the steamer swing round as Frithiof turned her.

'Going back to Cape Town?' said Keller.

Frithiof did not answer, but tore away at the wheel. Then he beckoned us three to help, and we held the wheel down till the *Rathmines* answered it, and we found ourselves looking into the white of our own wake, with the still oily sea tearing past our bows, though we were not going more than half steam ahead.

The captain stretched out his arm from the bridge and shouted. A minute later I would have given a great deal to have shouted too, for one-half of the sea seemed to shoulder itself above the other half; and came on in the shape of a hill. There was neither crest, comb, nor curl-over to it; nothing but black water with little waves chasing each other about the flanks. I saw it stream past and on a level with the *Rathmines*' bow-plates before the steamer hove up her bulk to rise, and I argued that this would be the last of all earthly voyages for me. Then we lifted for ever and ever and ever, till I heard Keller saying in my ear, 'The bowels of the deep, good Lord!' and the *Rathmines* stood poised, her screw racing and drumming on the slope of a hollow that stretched downwards for a good half-mile.

We went down that hollow, nose under for the most part, and the air smelt wet and muddy, like that of an emptied aquarium. There was a second hill to climb; I saw that much: but the water came aboard and carried me aft till it jammed me against the wheel-house door, and before I could catch breath or clear my eyes again we were rolling to and fro in torn water, with the scuppers pouring like eaves in a thunderstorm.

'There were three waves,' said Keller; 'and the stoke-hold's flooded.'

The firemen were on deck waiting, apparently, to be drowned. The engineer came and dragged them below, and the crew, gasping, began to work the clumsy Board of Trade pump. That showed nothing serious, and when I understood that the *Rathmines* was really on the water, and not beneath it, I asked what had happened.

'The captain says it was a blow-up under the sea – a volcano,' said Keller.

'It hasn't warmed anything,' I said. I was feeling bitterly cold, and cold was almost unknown in those waters. I went below to change my clothes, and when I came up everything was wiped out in clinging white fog.

'Are there going to be any more surprises?' said Keller to the captain.

'I don't know. Be thankful you're alive, gentlemen. That's a tidal wave thrown up by a volcano. Probably the bottom of the sea has been lifted a few feet somewhere or other. I can't quite understand this cold spell. Our sea-thermometer says the surface water is 44°, and it should be 68° at least.'

'It's abominable,' said Keller, shivering. 'But hadn't you better attend to the fog-horn? It seems to me that I heard something.'

'Heard! Good heavens!' said the captain from the bridge, ' I should think you did.' He pulled the string of our fog-horn, which was a weak one. It sputtered and choked, because the stoke-hold was full of water and the fires were half-drowned, and at last gave out a moan. It was answered from the fog by one of the most appalling steam-sirens I have ever heard. Keller turned as white as I did, for the fog, the cold fog, was upon us, and any man may be forgiven for fearing a death he cannot see.

'Give her steam there!' said the captain to the engine-room. 'Steam for the whistle, if we have to go dead slow.'

We bellowed again, and the damp dripped off the awnings on to the deck as we listened for the reply. It seemed to be astern this time, but much nearer than before.

'*The Pembroke Castle* on us!' said Keller; and then, viciously, 'Well, thank God, we shall sink her too.'

'It's a side-wheel steamer,' I whispered. 'Can't you hear the paddles?'

This time we whistled and roared till the steam gave out, and the answer nearly deafened us. There was a sound of frantic threshing in the water, apparently about fifty yards away, and something shot past in the whiteness that looked as though it were grey and red.

'The sea is bewitched,' said Frithiof from the wheel-house. 'There are two steamers!'

Another siren sounded on our bow, and the little steamer rolled in the wash of something that had passed unseen.

'We're evidently in the middle of a fleet,' said Keller quietly. 'If one doesn't run us down, the other will. Phew! What in creation is that?'

I sniffed, for there was a poisonous rank smell in the cold air – a smell that I had smelt before.

'If I was on land I should say that it was an alligator. It smells like musk,' I answered.

'Not ten thousand alligators could make that smell,' said Zuyland; 'I have smelt them.'

'Bewitched! Bewitched!' said Frithiof. 'The sea she is turned upside down, and we are walking along the bottom.'

Again the *Rathmines* rolled in the wash of some unseen ship, and a silver-grey wave broke over the bow, leaving on the deck a sheet of sediment – the grey broth that has its place in the fathomless deeps of the sea. A sprinkling of the wave fell on my face, and it was so cold that it stung as boiling water stings. The dead and most untouched deep water of the sea had been heaved to the top by the submarine volcano – the chill still water that kills all life and smells of desolation and emptiness. We did not need either the blinding fog or that indescribable smell of musk to make us unhappy – we were shivering with cold and wretchedness where we stood.

'The hot air on the cold water makes this fog,' said the captain; 'it ought to clear in a little time.'

'Whistle, oh! whistle, and let's get out of it,' said Keller.

The captain whistled again, and far and far astern the invisible twin steam-sirens answered us. Their blasting shriek grew louder, till at last it seemed to tear out of the fog just above our quarter, and I cowered while the *Rathmines* plunged bows under on a double swell that crossed.

'No more,' said Frithiof, 'it is not good any more. Let us get away, in the name of God.'

Keller opened his mouth to speak. The words died on his lips, his eyes began to start from his head, and his jaw fell. Some six or seven feet above the port bulwarks, framed in fog, and as utterly unsupported as the full moon, hung a face. It was not human, and it certainly was not animal, for it did not belong to this earth as known to man. The mouth was open, revealing a ridiculously tiny tongue – as absurd as the tongue of an elephant; there were tense wrinkles of white skin at the angles of the drawn lips, white feelers like those of a barbel sprung from the lower jaw, and there was no sign of teeth within the mouth. But the horror of the face lay in the eyes, for those were sightless – white, in sockets as white as scraped bone, and blind. Yet for all this the face, wrinkled as the mask of a lion is drawn in Assyrian sculpture, was alive with rage and terror. One long white feeler touched our bulwarks. Then the face disappeared with the swiftness of a blindworm popping into its burrow.

Keller came up to me, ashy white. He put his hand into his pocket, took a cigar, bit it, dropped it, thrust his shaking thumb into his mouth and mumbled, 'The giant gooseberry and the raining frogs! Gimme a light – gimme a light! Say, gimme a light.' A little bead of blood dropped from his thumb joint.

I respected the motive, though the manifestation was absurd.

'Stop, you'll bite your thumb off,' I said, and Keller laughed brokenly as he picked up his cigar. Only Zuyland, leaning over the port bulwarks, seemed self-possessed. He declared later that he was very sick.

'We've seen it,' he said, turning round. 'That is it.'

'What?' said Keller, chewing the unlighted cigar.

As he spoke the fog was blown into shreds, and we saw the sea, grey with mud, rolling on every side of us and empty of all life. Then in one spot it bubbled and became like the pot of ointment that the Bible speaks of. From that wide-ringed trouble a Thing came up – a grey and red Thing with a neck – a Thing that bellowed and writhed in pain. Frithiof drew in his breath and held it till the red letters of the ship's name, woven across his jersey, straggled and opened out as though they had been badly type set.

Then he said with a little cluck in his throat, 'Ah me! It is blind. That thing is blind,' and a murmur of pity went through us all, for we could see that the thing on the water was blind and in pain. Something had gashed and cut the great sides cruelly and the blood was spurting out. The grey ooze of the undermost sea lay in the monstrous wrinkles of the back, and poured away in sluices. The blind white head flung back and battered the wounds, and the body in its torment rose clear of the red and grey waves till we saw a pair of quivering shoulders streaked with weed and rough with shells, but as white in the clear spaces as the hairless, maneless, blind, toothless head. Afterwards, came a dot on the horizon and the sound of a shrill scream, and it was as though a shuttle shot all across the sea in one breath, and a second head and neck tore through the levels, driving a whispering wall of water to right and left. The two Things met – the one untouched and the other in its death-throe – male and female, we said, the female coming to the male. She circled round him bellowing, and laid her neck across the curve of his great turtle-back, and he disappeared under water for an instant, but flung up again, grunting in agony while the blood ran. Once the entire head and neck shot clear of the water and stiffened, and I heard Keller saying, as though he was watching a street accident, 'Give him air. For God's sake, give him air.' Then the death-struggle began, with crampings and twistings and jerkings of the white bulk to and fro, till our little steamer rolled again, and each grey wave coated her plates with the grey slime. The sun was clear, there was no wind, and we watched, the whole crew, stokers and all, in wonder and pity, but chiefly pity. The Thing was so helpless, and, save for his mate, so alone. No human eye should have beheld him. He had been spewed up, mangled and dying, from his rest on the sea-floor, where he might have lived till the Judgment Day, and we saw the tides of his life go from him as an angry tide goes out across rocks in the teeth of a landward gale. His mate lay rocking on the water a little distance off, bellowing continually, and the smell of musk came down upon the ship making us cough.

At last the battle for life ended in a batter of coloured seas. We saw the writhing neck fall like a flail, the carcass turn sideways, showing the glint of a white belly and the inset of a gigantic hind leg or flipper. Then all sank, and sea boiled over it, while the mate swam round and round, darting her head in every direction. Though we might have feared that she would attack the steamer, no power on earth could have drawn any one of us from our places that hour. We watched, holding our breaths. The mate paused in her search; we could hear the wash beating along her sides; reared her neck as high as she could reach, blind and lonely in all that loneliness of the sea, and sent one desperate bellow booming across the swells as an oyster-shell skips across a pond. Then she made off to the westward, the sun shining on the white head and the wake behind it, till nothing was left to see but a little pin point of silver on the horizon. We stood on our course again; and the *Rathmines*, coated with the sea-sediment from bow to stern, looked like a ship made grey with terror.

***

'We must pool our notes,' was the first coherent remark from Keller. 'We're three trained journalists – we hold absolutely the biggest scoop on record.'

I objected to this. Nothing is gained by collaboration in journalism when all deal with the same facts, so we went to work each according to his own lights.

Keller was insolent with joy. He was going to cable from Southampton to the New York *World,* mail his account to America on the same day, paralyse London with his three columns of loosely knitted headlines, and generally efface the earth. 'You'll see how I work a big scoop when I get it,' he said.

'Is this your first visit to England?' I asked.

'Yes,' said he. 'You don't seem to appreciate the beauty of our scoop. It's pyramidal – the death of the sea-serpent! Good heavens alive, man, it's the biggest thing ever vouchsafed to a paper!'

'Curious to think that it will never appear in any paper, isn't it?' I said.

Zuyland was near me, and he nodded quickly.

'What do you mean?' said Keller. 'If you're enough of a Britisher to throw this thing away, I shan't. I thought you were a newspaper man.'

'I am. That's why I know. Don't be an ass, Keller. Remember, I'm seven hundred years your senior, and what your grandchildren may learn five hundred years hence, I learned from my grandfathers about five hundred years ago. You won't do it, because you can't.'

This conversation was held in open sea, where everything seems possible, some hundred miles from Southampton. We passed the Needles Light at dawn, and the lifting day showed the stucco villas on the green and the awful orderliness of England – line upon line, wall upon wall, solid stone dock and monolithic pier. We waited an hour in the Customs shed, and there was ample time for the effect to soak in.

I heard Keller gasp as the influence of the land closed about him. Zuyland had torn up his account and thrown it overboard that morning early. His reasons were my reasons.

In the train Keller began to revise his copy, and every time that he looked at the trim little fields, the red villas, and the embankments of the line, the blue pencil plunged remorselessly through the slips. He appeared to have dredged the dictionary for adjectives. I could think of none that he had not used.

'Aren't you going to leave him a single bellow?' I asked sympathetically. 'Remember, everything goes in the States.'

'That's just the curse of it,' said Keller below his breath. 'We've played 'em for suckers so often that when it comes to the golden truth — I'd like to try this on a London paper. You have first call there, though.'

'Not in the least. I'm not touching the thing in our papers. I shall be happy to leave 'em all to you; but surely you'll cable it home?'

'No. Not if I can make the scoop here and see the Britishers sit up.'

***

When we reached London Keller disappeared in the direction of the Strand. What his experiences may have been I cannot tell, but it seems that he invaded the office of an evening paper at 11.45 a.m. (I told him English editors were most idle at that hour), and mentioned my name as that of a witness to the truth of his story.

'I was nearly fired out,' he said furiously at lunch. 'As soon as I mentioned you, the old man said that I was to tell you that they didn't want any more of your practical jokes, and that you knew the hours to call if you had anything to sell, and that they'd see you condemned before they helped to puff one of your infernal yarns in advance. Say, what record do you hold for truth in this country, anyway?'

'A beauty. You ran up against it, that's all. Why don't you leave the English papers alone and cable to New York? Everything goes over there.'

'Can't you see that's just why?' he repeated.

'I saw it a long time ago. You don't intend to cable, then?'

'Yes, I do,' he answered, in the over-emphatic voice of one who does not know his own mind.

That afternoon I walked him abroad and about, over the streets that run between the pavements like channels of grooved and tongued lava, over the bridges that are made of enduring stone, through subways floored and sided with yard-thick concrete, between houses that are never rebuilt, and by river-steps hewn, to the eye, from the living rock. A black fog chased us into Westminster Abbey, and, standing there in the darkness, I could hear the wings of the dead centuries circling round the head of Litchfield A. Keller, journalist, of Dayton, Ohio, U.S.A., whose mission it was to make the Britishers sit up.

He stumbled gasping into the thick gloom, and the roar of the traffic came to his bewildered ears.

'Let's go to the telegraph-office and cable,' I said. 'Can't you hear the New York *World* crying for news of the great sea-serpent, blind, white, and smelling of musk, stricken to death by a submarine volcano, and assisted by his loving wife to die in mid-ocean, as visualised by an American citizen, the breezy, newsy, brainy newspaper man of Dayton, Ohio?'

'You've got me on your own ground,' said he, tugging at his overcoat pocket. He pulled out his copy, with the cable forms – for he had written out his telegram – and put them all into my hand, groaning, 'I pass.'

'Never mind, Keller. It isn't your fault. It's the fault of your country. If you had been seven hundred years older you'd have done what I am going to do.'

'What are you going to do?'

'Tell it as a lie.'

'Fiction?' This with the full-blooded disgust of a journalist for the illegitimate branch of the profession.

'You can call it that if you like. I shall call it a lie.'

And a lie it has become.

SUBHA

RABINDRANATH TAGORE

> Rabindranath Tagore (1861-1941) wrote poetry and short stories based largely around rural life in the Bengal region of India in which he lived. 'Subha' was first published in 1898, when most Indians lived in the countryside, with little money and few possessions. At that time, many Indians could not read or write, a point of significance in this story.
>
> Tagore, who won the Nobel Prize for Literature in 1913, is still revered in Bengal, an area of India well known for holding its intellectual figures in high regard.

When the girl was given the name of Subhashini, who could have guessed that she would prove dumb? Her two elder sisters were Sukeshini and Suhasini, and for the sake of uniformity her father named his youngest girl Subhashini. She was called Subha for short.

Her two elder sisters had been married with the usual cost and difficulty, and now the youngest daughter lay like a silent weight upon the heart of her parents. All the world seemed to think that, because she did not speak, therefore she did not feel; it discussed her future and its own anxiety freely in her presence. She had understood from her earliest childhood that God had sent her like a curse to her father's house, so she withdrew herself from ordinary people and tried to live apart. If only they would all forget her she felt she could endure it. But who can forget pain? Night and day her parents' minds were aching on her account. Especially her mother looked upon her as a deformity in herself. To a mother a daughter is a more closely intimate part of herself than a son can be; and a fault in her is a source of personal shame. Banikantha, Subha's father, loved her rather better than his other daughters; her mother regarded her with aversion as a stain upon her own body.

If Subha lacked speech, she did not lack a pair of large dark eyes, shaded with long lashes; and her lips trembled like a leaf in response to any thought that rose in her mind.

When we express our thought in words, the medium is not found easily. There must be a process of translation, which is often inexact, and then we fall into error. But black eyes need no translating; the mind itself throws a shadow upon them. In them thought opens or shuts, shines forth or goes out in darkness, hangs steadfast like the setting moon or like the swift and restless lightning illumines all quarters of the sky. They who from birth have had no other speech than the trembling of their lips learn a language of the eyes, endless in expression, deep as the sea, clear as the heavens, wherein play dawn and sunset, light and shadow. The dumb have a lonely grandeur like Nature's own. Wherefore the other children almost dreaded Subha and never played with her. She was silent and companionless as noontide. **II**

The hamlet where she lived was Chandipur. Its river, small for a river of Bengal, kept to its narrow bounds like a daughter of the middle class. This busy streak of water never overflowed its banks, but went about its duties as though it were a member of every family in the villages beside it. On either side were houses and banks shaded with trees. So stepping from her queenly throne, the river-goddess became a garden deity of each home, and forgetful of herself performed her task of endless benediction with swift and cheerful foot.

Banikantha's house looked out upon the stream. Every hut and stack in the place could be seen by the passing boatmen. I know not if amid these signs of worldly wealth any one noticed the little girl who, when her work was done, stole away to the waterside and sat there. But here Nature fulfilled her want of speech and spoke for her. The murmur of the brook, the voice of the village folk, the songs of the boatmen, the crying of the birds and rustle of trees mingled and were one with the trembling of her heart. They became one vast wave of sound which beat upon her restless soul. This murmur and movement of Nature were the dumb girl's language; that speech of the dark eyes, which the long lashes shaded, was the language of the world about her. From the trees, where the cicalas chirped, to the quiet stars there was nothing but signs and gestures, weeping and sighing. And in the deep mid-noon, when the boatmen and fisher-folk had gone to their dinner, when the villagers slept and birds were still, when the ferry-boats were idle, when the great busy world paused in its toil and became suddenly a lonely, awful giant, then beneath the vast impressive heavens there were only dumb Nature and a dumb girl, sitting very silent – one under the spreading sunlight, the other where a small tree cast its shadow.

But Subha was not altogether without friends. In the stall were two cows, Sarbbashi and Panguli. They had never heard their names from her lips, but they knew her footfall. Though she had no words, she murmured lovingly and they understood her gentle murmuring better than all speech. When she fondled them or scolded or coaxed them, they understood her better than men could do. Subha would come to the shed and throw her arms round Sarbbashi's neck; she would rub her cheek against her friend's, and Panguli would turn her great kind eyes and lick her face. The girl paid them three regular visits every day and others that were irregular. Whenever she heard any words that hurt her, she would come to these dumb friends out of due time. It was as though they guessed her anguish of spirit from her quiet look of sadness. Coming close to her, they would rub their horns softly against her arms, and in dumb, puzzled fashion try to comfort her. Besides these two, there were goats and a kitten; but Subha had not the same equality of friendship with them, though they showed the same attachment. Every time it got a chance, night or day, the kitten would jump into her lap, and settle down to slumber, and show its appreciation of an aid to sleep as Subha drew her soft fingers over its neck and back.

Subha had a comrade also among the higher animals, and it is hard to say what were the girl's relations with him; for he could speak, and his gift of speech left them without any common language. He was the youngest boy of the Gosains, Pratap by name, an idle fellow. After long effort, his parents had abandoned the hope that he would ever make his living. Now losels have this advantage, that, though their own folk disapprove of them, they are generally popular with every one else. Having no work to chain them, they become public property. Just as every town needs an open space where all may breathe, so a village needs two or three gentlemen of leisure, who can give time to all; then, if we are lazy and want a companion, one is to hand.

Pratap's chief ambition was to catch fish. He managed to waste a lot of time this way, and might be seen almost any afternoon so employed. It was thus most often that he met Subha. Whatever he was about, he liked a companion; and, when one is catching fish, a silent companion is best of all. Pratap respected Subha for her taciturnity, and, as every one called her Subha, he showed his affection by calling her Su. Subha used to sit beneath a tamarind, and Pratap, a little distance off, would cast his line. Pratap took with him a small allowance of betel, and Subha prepared it for him. And I think that, sitting and gazing a long while, she desired ardently to bring some great help to Pratap, to be of real aid, to prove by any means that she was not a useless burden to the world. But there was nothing to do. Then she turned to the Creator in prayer for some rare power, that by an astonishing miracle she might startle Pratap into exclaiming: 'My! I never dreamt our Su could have done this!'

Only think, if Subha had been a water nymph, she might have risen slowly from the river, bringing the gem of a snake's crown to the landing-place. Then Pratap, leaving his paltry fishing, might dive into the lower world, and see there, on a golden bed in a palace of silver, whom else but dumb little Su, Banikantha's child? Yes, our Su, the only daughter of the king of that shining city of jewels! But that might not be, it was impossible. Not that anything is really impossible, but Su had been born, not into the royal house of Patalpur, but into Banikantha's family, and she knew no means of astonishing the Gosains' boy.

Gradually she grew up. Gradually she began to find herself. A new inexpressible consciousness like a tide from the central places of the sea, when the moon is full, swept through her. She saw herself, questioned herself, but no answer came that she could understand.

Once upon a time, late on a night of full moon, she slowly opened her door and peeped out timidly. Nature, herself at full moon, like lonely Subha, was looking down on the sleeping earth. Her strong young life beat within her; joy and sadness filled her being to its brim; she reached the limits even of her own illimitable loneliness, nay, passed beyond them. Her heart was heavy, and she could not speak. At the skirts of this silent troubled Mother there stood a silent troubled girl. ∎

The thought of her marriage filled her parents with an anxious care. People blamed them, and even talked of making them outcasts. Banikantha was well off; they had fish-curry twice daily; and consequently he did not lack enemies. Then the women interfered, and Bani went away for a few days. Presently he returned and said: 'We must go to Calcutta.'

They got ready to go to this strange country. Subha's heart was heavy with tears, like a mist-wrapt dawn. With a vague fear that had been gathering for days, she dogged her father and mother like a dumb animal. With her large eyes wide open, she scanned their faces as though she wished to learn something. But not a word did they vouchsafe. One afternoon in the midst of all this, as Pratap was fishing, he laughed: 'So then, Su, they have caught your bridegroom, and you are going to be married! Mind you don't forget me altogether!' Then he turned his mind again to his fish. As a stricken doe looks in the hunter's face, asking in silent agony: 'What have I done to you?' so Subha looked at Pratap. That day she sat no longer beneath her tree. Banikantha, having finished his nap, was smoking in his bedroom when Subha dropped down at his feet and burst out weeping as she gazed towards him. Banikantha tried to comfort her, and his cheek grew wet with tears.

It was settled that on the morrow they should go to Calcutta. Subha went to the cowshed to bid farewell to her childhood's comrades. She fed them with her hand; she clasped their necks; she looked into their faces, and tears fell fast from the eyes which spoke for her. That night was the tenth of the moon. Subha left her room, and flung herself down on her grassy couch beside her dear river. It was as if she threw her arms about Earth, her strong silent mother, and tried to say: 'Do not let me leave you, mother. Put your arms about me, as I have put mine about you, and hold me fast.'

One day in a house in Calcutta, Subha's mother dressed her up with great care. She imprisoned her hair, knotting it up in laces, she hung her about with ornaments, and did her best to kill her natural beauty. Subha's eyes filled with tears. Her mother, fearing they would grow swollen with weeping, scolded her harshly, but the tears disregarded the scolding. The bridegroom came with a friend to inspect the bride. Her parents were dizzy with anxiety and fear when they saw the god arrive to select the beast for his sacrifice. Behind the stage, the mother called her instructions aloud, and increased her daughter's weeping twofold, before she sent her into the examiner's presence. The great man, after scanning her a long time, observed: 'Not so bad.'

He took special note of her tears, and thought she must have a tender heart. He put it to her credit in the account, arguing that the heart, which today was distressed at leaving her parents, would presently prove a useful possession. Like the oyster's pearls, the child's tears only increased her value, and he made no other comment.

The almanac was consulted, and the marriage took place on an auspicious day. Having delivered over their dumb girl into another's hands, Subha's parents returned home. Thank God! Their caste in this and their safety in the next world were assured! The bridegroom's work lay in the west, and shortly after the marriage he took his wife thither.

In less than ten days every one knew that the bride was dumb! At least, if any one did not, it was not her fault, for she deceived no one. Her eyes told them everything, though no one understood her. She looked on every hand, she found no speech, she missed the faces, familiar from birth, of those who had understood a dumb girl's language. In her silent heart there sounded an endless, voiceless weeping, which only the Searcher of Hearts could hear.

THE OPEN WINDOW

SAKI

The writer is **Hector Hugh Munro** (1870-1916), a British writer, who used the pen name **Saki**. His stories often poked fun at middle and upper class Edwardian society. 'The Open Window' was first published in the collection *Beasts and Super-Beasts* in 1914.

'My aunt will be down presently, Mr. Nuttel,' said a very self-possessed young lady of fifteen; 'in the meantime you must try and put up with me.'

Framton Nuttel endeavoured to say the correct something which should duly flatter the niece of the moment without unduly discounting the aunt that was to come. Privately he doubted more than ever whether these formal visits on a succession of total strangers would do much towards helping the nerve cure which he was supposed to be undergoing.

'I know how it will be,' his sister had said when he was preparing to migrate to this rural retreat; 'you will bury yourself down there and not speak to a living soul, and your nerves will be worse than ever from moping. I shall just give you letters of introduction to all the people I know there. Some of them, as far as I can remember, were quite nice.'

Framton wondered whether Mrs. Sappleton, the lady to whom he was presenting one of the letters of introduction came into the nice division.

'Do you know many of the people round here?' asked the niece, when she judged that they had had sufficient silent communion.

'Hardly a soul,' said Framton. 'My sister was staying here, at the rectory, you know, some four years ago, and she gave me letters of introduction to some of the people here.'

He made the last statement in a tone of distinct regret.

'Then you know practically nothing about my aunt?' pursued the self-possessed young lady.

'Only her name and address,' admitted the caller. He was wondering whether Mrs. Sappleton was in the married or widowed state. An indefinable something about the room seemed to suggest masculine habitation.

'Her great tragedy happened just three years ago,' said the child; 'that would be since your sister's time.'

'Her tragedy?' asked Framton; somehow in this restful country spot tragedies seemed out of place.

'You may wonder why we keep that window wide open on an October afternoon,' said the niece, indicating a large French window that opened on to a lawn.

'It is quite warm for the time of the year,' said Framton; 'but has that window got anything to do with the tragedy?'

'Out through that window, three years ago to a day, her husband and her two young brothers went off for their day's shooting. They never came back. In crossing the moor to their favourite snipe-shooting ground they were all three engulfed in a treacherous piece of bog. It had been that dreadful wet summer, you know, and places that were safe in other years gave way suddenly without warning. Their bodies were never recovered. That was the dreadful part of it.' Here the child's voice lost its self-possessed note and became falteringly human. 'Poor aunt always thinks that they will come back someday, they and the little brown spaniel that was lost with them, and walk in at that window just as they used to do. That is why the window is kept open every evening till it is quite dusk. Poor dear aunt, she has often told me how they went out, her husband with his white waterproof coat over his arm, and Ronnie, her youngest brother, singing 'Bertie, why do you bound?' as he always did to tease her, because she said it got on her nerves. Do you know, sometimes on still, quiet evenings like this, I almost get a creepy feeling that they will all walk in through that window –'

She broke off with a little shudder. It was a relief to Framton when the aunt bustled into the room with a whirl of apologies for being late in making her appearance.

'I hope Vera has been amusing you?' she said.

'She has been very interesting,' said Framton.

'I hope you don't mind the open window,' said Mrs. Sappleton briskly; 'my husband and brothers will be home directly from shooting, and they always come in this way. They've been out for snipe in the marshes today, so they'll make a fine mess over my poor carpets. So like you menfolk, isn't it?'

She rattled on cheerfully about the shooting and the scarcity of birds, and the prospects for duck in the winter. To Framton it was all purely horrible. He made a desperate but only partially successful effort to turn the talk on to a less ghastly topic, he was conscious that his hostess was giving him only a fragment of her attention, and her eyes were constantly straying past him to the open window and the lawn beyond. It was certainly an unfortunate coincidence that he should have paid his visit on this tragic anniversary.

'The doctors agree in ordering me complete rest, an absence of mental excitement, and avoidance of anything in the nature of violent physical exercise,' announced Framton, who laboured under the tolerably widespread delusion that total strangers and chance acquaintances are hungry for the least detail of one's ailments and infirmities, their cause and cure. 'On the matter of diet they are not so much in agreement,' he continued.

'No?' said Mrs. Sappleton, in a voice which only replaced a yawn at the last moment. Then she suddenly brightened into alert attention – but not to what Framton was saying.

'Here they are at last!' she cried. 'Just in time for tea, and don't they look as if they were muddy up to the eyes!'

Framton shivered slightly and turned towards the niece with a look intended to convey sympathetic comprehension. The child was staring out through the open window with a dazed horror in her eyes. In a chill shock of nameless fear Framton swung round in his seat and looked in the same direction.

In the deepening twilight three figures were walking across the lawn towards the window, they all carried guns under their arms, and one of them was additionally burdened with a white coat hung over his shoulders. A tired brown spaniel kept close at their heels. Noiselessly they neared the house, and then a hoarse young voice chanted out of the dusk: 'I said, Bertie, why do you bound?'

Framton grabbed wildly at his stick and hat; the hall door, the gravel drive, and the front gate were dimly noted stages in his headlong retreat. A cyclist coming along the road had to run into the hedge to avoid imminent collision.

'Here we are, my dear,' said the bearer of the white mackintosh, coming in through the window, 'fairly muddy, but most of it's dry. Who was that who bolted out as we came up?'

'A most extraordinary man, a Mr. Nuttel,' said Mrs. Sappleton; 'could only talk about his illnesses, and dashed off without a word of goodbye or apology when you arrived. One would think he had seen a ghost.'

'I expect it was the spaniel,' said the niece calmly; 'he told me he had a horror of dogs. He was once hunted into a cemetery somewhere on the banks of the Ganges by a pack of pariah dogs, and had to spend the night in a newly dug grave with the creatures snarling and grinning and foaming just above him. Enough to make anyone lose their nerve.'

Romance at short notice was her speciality.

A CUP OF TEA

KATHERINE MANSFIELD

> **Katherine Mansfield** (1888-1923) was born in New Zealand, moving to London in 1903. She led a Bohemian lifestyle, mixing in artistic circles and travelling widely around Europe. However, she contracted tuberculosis in 1917, which put an end to this lifestyle and led to her early death.
>
> She is well known for her short stories and is said to have influenced one of the most famous English writers of the early 20th century, Virginia Woolf.
>
> 'A Cup of Tea', first published in 1922, is a good example of how she explores the problems faced by women of her generation.

Rosemary Fell was not exactly beautiful. No, you couldn't have called her beautiful. Pretty? Well, if you took her to pieces... But why be so cruel as to take anyone to pieces? She was young, brilliant, extremely modern, exquisitely well dressed, amazingly well read in the newest of the new books, and her parties were the most delicious mixture of the really important people and... artists – quaint creatures, discoveries of hers, some of them too terrifying for words, but others quite presentable and amusing.

Rosemary had been married two years. She had a duck of a boy. No, not Peter – Michael. And her husband absolutely adored her. They were rich, really rich, not just comfortably well off, which is odious and stuffy and sounds like one's grandparents. But if Rosemary wanted to shop she would go to Paris as you and I would go to Bond Street. If she wanted to buy flowers, the car pulled up at that perfect shop in Regent Street, and

Rosemary inside the shop just gazed in her dazzled, rather exotic way, and said: 'I want those and those and those. Give me four bunches of those. And that jar of roses. Yes, I'll have all the roses in the jar. No, no lilac. I hate lilac. It's got no shape.' The attendant bowed and put the lilac out of sight, as though this was only too true; lilac was dreadfully shapeless. 'Give me those stumpy little tulips. Those red and white ones.' And she was followed to the car by a thin shop-girl staggering under an immense white paper armful that looked like a baby in long clothes...

One winter afternoon she had been buying something in a little antique shop in Curzon Street. It was a shop she liked. For one thing, one usually had it to oneself. And then the man who kept it was ridiculously fond of serving her. He beamed whenever she came in. He clasped his hands; he was so gratified he could scarcely speak. Flattery, of course. All the same, there was something...

'You see, madam,' he would explain in his low respectful tones, 'I love my things. I would rather not part with them than sell them to someone who does not appreciate them, who has not that fine feeling which is so rare...' And, breathing deeply, he unrolled a tiny square of blue velvet and pressed it on the glass counter with his pale finger-tips.

Today it was a little box. He had been keeping it for her. He had shown it to nobody as yet. An exquisite little enamel box with a glaze so fine it looked as though it had been baked in cream. On the lid a minute creature stood under a flowery tree, and a more minute creature still had her arms round his neck. Her hat, really no bigger than a geranium petal, hung from a branch; it had green ribbons. And there was a pink cloud like a watchful cherub floating above their heads. Rosemary took her hands out of her long gloves. She always took off her gloves to examine such things. Yes, she liked it very much. She loved it; it was a great duck. She must have it. And, turning the creamy box, opening and shutting it, she couldn't help noticing how charming her hands were against the blue velvet. The shopman, in some dim cavern of his mind, may have dared to think so too. For he took a pencil, leant over the counter, and his pale, bloodless fingers crept timidly towards those rosy, flashing ones, as he murmured gently: 'If I may venture to point out to madam, the flowers on the little lady's bodice.'

'Charming!' Rosemary admired the flowers. But what was the price? For a moment the shopman did not seem to hear. Then a murmur reached her.

'Twenty-eight guineas, madam.'

'Twenty-eight guineas.' Rosemary gave no sign. She laid the little box down; she buttoned her gloves again. Twenty-eight guineas. Even if one is rich... She looked vague. She stared at a plump tea-kettle like a plump hen above the shopman's head, and her voice was dreamy as she answered: 'Well, keep it for me – will you? I'll...'

But the shopman had already bowed as though keeping it for her was all any human being could ask. He would be willing, of course, to keep it for her for ever.

The discreet door shut with a click. She was outside on the step, gazing at the winter afternoon. Rain was falling, and with the rain it seemed the dark came too, spinning down like ashes. There was a cold bitter taste in the air, and the new-lighted lamps looked sad. Sad were the lights in the houses opposite. Dimly they burned as if regretting something. And people hurried by, hidden under their hateful umbrellas. Rosemary felt a strange pang. She pressed her muff against her breast; she wished she had the little box, too, to cling to. Of course, the car was there. She'd only to cross the pavement. But still she waited. There are moments, horrible moments in life, when one emerges from shelter and looks out, and it's awful. One oughtn't to give way to them. One ought to go home and have an extra-special tea. But at the very instant of thinking that, a young girl, thin, dark, shadowy – where had she come from? – was standing at Rosemary's elbow and a voice like a sigh, almost like a sob, breathed: 'Madam, may I speak to you a moment?'

'Speak to me?' Rosemary turned. She saw a little battered creature with enormous eyes, someone quite young, no older than herself, who clutched at her coat-collar with reddened hands, and shivered as though she had just come out of the water.

'M-madam,' stammered the voice. 'Would you let me have the price of a cup of tea?'

'A cup of tea?' There was something simple, sincere in that voice; it wasn't in the least the voice of a beggar. 'Then have you no money at all?' asked Rosemary.

'None, madam,' came the answer.

'How extraordinary!' Rosemary peered through the dusk, and the girl gazed back at her. How more than extraordinary! And suddenly it seemed to Rosemary such an adventure. It was like something out of a novel by Dostoevsky, this meeting in the dusk. Supposing she took the girl home? Supposing she did do one of those things she was always reading about or seeing on the stage, what would happen? It would be thrilling. And she heard herself saying afterwards to the amazement of her friends: 'I simply took her home with me,' as she stepped forward and said to that dim person beside her: 'Come home to tea with me.'

The girl drew back startled. She even stopped shivering for a moment. Rosemary put out a hand and touched her arm. 'I mean it,' she said, smiling. And she felt how simple and kind her smile was. 'Why won't you? Do. Come home with me now in my car and have tea.'

'You – you don't mean it, madam,' said the girl, and there was pain in her voice.

'But I do,' cried Rosemary. 'I want you to. To please me. Come along.'

The girl put her fingers to her lips and her eyes devoured Rosemary. 'You're – you're not taking me to the police station?' she stammered.

'The police station!' Rosemary laughed out. 'Why should I be so cruel? No, I only want to make you warm and to hear – anything you care to tell me.'

Hungry people are easily led. The footman held the door of the car open, and a moment later they were skimming through the dusk.

'There!' said Rosemary. She had a feeling of triumph as she slipped her hand through the velvet strap. She could have said, 'Now I've got you,' as she gazed at the little captive she had netted. But of course she meant it kindly. Oh, more than kindly. She was going to prove to this girl that – wonderful things did happen in life, that – fairy godmothers were real, that – rich people had hearts, and that women were sisters. She turned impulsively, saying, 'Don't be frightened. After all, why shouldn't you come back with me? We're both women. If I'm the more fortunate, you ought to expect…' ∎

But happily at that moment, for she didn't know how the sentence was going to end, the car stopped. The bell was rung, the door opened, and with a charming, protecting, almost embracing movement, Rosemary drew the other into the hall. Warmth, softness, light, a sweet scent, all those things so familiar to her she never even thought about them, she watched that other receive. It was fascinating. She was like the rich little girl in her nursery with all the cupboards to open, all the boxes to unpack.

'Come, come upstairs,' said Rosemary, longing to begin to be generous. 'Come up to my room.' And, besides, she wanted to spare this poor little thing from being stared at by the servants; she decided as they mounted the stairs she would not even ring to Jeanne, but take off her things by herself. The great thing was to be natural!

And 'There!' cried Rosemary again, as they reached her beautiful big bedroom with the curtains drawn, the fire leaping on her wonderful lacquer furniture, her gold cushions and the primrose and blue rugs.

The girl stood just inside the door; she seemed dazed. But Rosemary didn't mind that.

'Come and sit down,' she cried, dragging her big chair up to the fire, 'in this comfy chair. Come and get warm. You look so dreadfully cold.'

'I daren't, madam,' said the girl, and she edged backwards.

'Oh, please,' – Rosemary ran forward – 'you mustn't be frightened, you mustn't, really. Sit down, and when I've taken off my things we shall go into the next room and have tea and be cosy. Why are you afraid?' And gently she half pushed the thin figure into its deep cradle.

But there was no answer. The girl stayed just as she had been put, with her hands by her sides and her mouth slightly open. To be quite sincere, she looked rather stupid. But Rosemary wouldn't acknowledge it. She leant over her, saying: 'Won't you take off your hat? Your pretty hair is all wet. And one is so much more comfortable without a hat, isn't one?'

There was a whisper that sounded like 'Very good, madam,' and the crushed hat was taken off.

'And let me help you off with your coat, too,' said Rosemary.

The girl stood up. But she held on to the chair with one hand and let Rosemary pull. It was quite an effort. The other scarcely helped her at all. She seemed to stagger like a child, and the thought came and went through

Rosemary's mind, that if people wanted helping they must respond a little, just a little, otherwise it became very difficult indeed. And what was she to do with the coat now? She left it on the floor, and the hat too. She was just going to take a cigarette off the mantelpiece when the girl said quickly, but so lightly and strangely: 'I'm very sorry, madam, but I'm going to faint. I shall go off, madam, if I don't have something.'

'Good heavens, how thoughtless I am!' Rosemary rushed to the bell.

'Tea! Tea at once! And some brandy immediately!'

The maid was gone again, but the girl almost cried out: 'No, I don't want no brandy. I never drink brandy. It's a cup of tea I want, madam.' And she burst into tears.

It was a terrible and fascinating moment. Rosemary knelt beside her chair.

'Don't cry, poor little thing,' she said. 'Don't cry.' And she gave the other her lace handkerchief. She really was touched beyond words. She put her arm round those thin, bird-like shoulders.

Now at last the other forgot to be shy, forgot everything except that they were both women, and gasped out: 'I can't go on no longer like this. I can't bear it. I can't bear it. I shall do away with myself. I can't bear no more.'

'You shan't have to. I'll look after you. Don't cry any more. Don't you see what a good thing it was that you met me? We'll have tea and you'll tell me everything. And I shall arrange something. I promise. Do stop crying. It's so exhausting. Please!'

The other did stop just in time for Rosemary to get up before the tea came. She had the table placed between them. She plied the poor little creature with everything, all the sandwiches, all the bread and butter, and every time her cup was empty she filled it with tea, cream and sugar. People always said sugar was so nourishing. As for herself she didn't eat; she smoked and looked away tactfully so that the other should not be shy.

And really the effect of that slight meal was marvellous. When the tea-table was carried away a new being, a light, frail creature with tangled hair, dark lips, deep, lighted eyes, lay back in the big chair in a kind of sweet languor, looking at the blaze. Rosemary lit a fresh cigarette; it was time to begin.

'And when did you have your last meal?' she asked softly.

But at that moment the door-handle turned.

'Rosemary, may I come in?' It was Philip.

'Of course.'

He came in. 'Oh, I'm so sorry,' he said, and stopped and stared.

'It's quite all right,' said Rosemary, smiling. 'This is my friend, Miss – '

'Smith, madam,' said the languid figure, who was strangely still and unafraid.

'Smith,' said Rosemary. 'We are going to have a little talk.'

'Oh yes,' said Philip. 'Quite,' and his eye caught sight of the coat and hat on the floor. He came over to the fire and turned his back to it. 'It's a beastly afternoon,' he said curiously, still looking at that listless figure, looking at its hands and boots, and then at Rosemary again.

'Yes, isn't it?' said Rosemary enthusiastically. 'Vile.'

Philip smiled his charming smile. 'As a matter of fact,' said he, 'I wanted you to come into the library for a moment. Would you? Will Miss Smith excuse us?'

The big eyes were raised to him, but Rosemary answered for her: 'Of course she will.' And they went out of the room together.

'I say,' said Philip, when they were alone. 'Explain. Who is she? What does it all mean?'

Rosemary, laughing, leaned against the door and said: 'I picked her up in Curzon Street. Really. She's a real pick-up. She asked me for the price of a cup of tea, and I brought her home with me.'

'But what on earth are you going to do with her?' cried Philip.

'Be nice to her,' said Rosemary quickly. 'Be frightfully nice to her. Look after her. I don't know how. We haven't talked yet. But show her – treat her – make her feel -'

'My darling girl,' said Philip, 'you're quite mad, you know. It simply can't be done.'

'I knew you'd say that,' retorted Rosemary. 'Why not? I want to. Isn't that a reason? And besides, one's always reading about these things. I decided -'

'But,' said Philip slowly, and he cut the end of a cigar, 'she's so astonishingly pretty.'

'Pretty?' Rosemary was so surprised that she blushed. 'Do you think so? I – I hadn't thought about it.'

'Good Lord!' Philip struck a match. 'She's absolutely lovely. Look again, my child. I was bowled over when I came into your room just now. However... I think you're making a ghastly mistake. Sorry, darling, if I'm crude and all that. But let me know if Miss Smith is going to dine with us in time for me to look up The Milliner's Gazette.'

'You absurd creature!' said Rosemary, and she went out of the library, but not back to her bedroom. She went to her writing-room and sat down at her desk. Pretty! Absolutely lovely! Bowled over! Her heart beat like a heavy bell. Pretty! Lovely! She drew her cheque-book towards her. But no, cheques would be no use, of course. She opened a drawer and took out five pound notes, looked at them, put two back, and holding the three squeezed in her hand, she went back to her bedroom.

Half an hour later Philip was still in the library, when Rosemary came in.

'I only wanted to tell you,' said she, and she leaned against the door again and looked at him with her dazzled exotic gaze, 'Miss Smith won't dine with us tonight.'

Philip put down the paper. 'Oh, what's happened? Previous engagement?'

Rosemary came over and sat down on his knee. 'She insisted on going,' said she, 'so I gave the poor little thing a present of money. I couldn't keep her against her will, could I?' she added softly.

Rosemary had just done her hair, darkened her eyes a little, and put on her pearls. She put up her hands and touched Philip's cheeks.

'Do you like me?' said she, and her tone, sweet, husky, troubled him.

'I like you awfully,' he said, and he held her tighter. 'Kiss me.'

There was a pause.

Then Rosemary said dreamily: 'I saw a fascinating little box today. It cost twenty-eight guineas. May I have it?'

Philip jumped her on his knee. 'You may, little wasteful one,' said he.

But that was not really what Rosemary wanted to say.

'Philip,' she whispered, and she pressed his head against her bosom, 'am I pretty?'

OLD MRS CHUNDLE

THOMAS HARDY

> 'Old Mrs Chundle' was written by **Thomas Hardy** (1840-1928), a famous British writer. Although he wrote the story in the 1880s, it was not published until 1929, after his death. This seems to have been because it was based on a real story and Hardy was worried about offending the people involved.
>
> You will find that Mrs Chundle speaks in Dorset dialect. You may find it easier to understand what she is saying if you listen as the story is read aloud.

The curate had not been a week in the parish, but the autumn morning proving fine he thought he would make a little water-colour sketch, showing a distant view of the Corvsgate ruin two miles off, which he had passed on his way hither. The sketch occupied him a longer time than he had anticipated. The luncheon hour drew on, and he felt hungry.

Quite near him was a stone-built old cottage of respectable and substantial build. He entered it, and was received by an old woman.

'Can you give me something to eat, my good woman?' he said.

She held her hand to her ear.

'Can you give me something for lunch?' he shouted. 'Bread-and-cheese – anything will do.'

A sour look crossed her face, and she shook her head. 'That's unlucky,' murmured he.

She reflected and said more urbanely: 'Well, I'm going to have my own bit o' dinner in no such long time hence. 'Tis taters and cabbage, boiled with a scantling o' bacon. Would ye like it? But I suppose 'tis the wrong sort, and that ye would sooner have bread-and-cheese?'

'No, I'll join you. Call me when it is ready. I'm just out here.'

'Ay, I've seen ye. Drawing the old stones, baint ye? Sure 'tis well some folk have nothing better to do with their time. Very well. I'll call ye, when I've dished up.'

He went out and resumed his painting; till in about seven or ten minutes the old woman appeared at her door and held up her hand. The curate washed his brush, went to the brook, rinsed his hands and proceeded to the house.

'There's yours,' she said, pointing to the table. 'I'll have my bit here.' And she denoted the settle.

'Why not join me?'

'Oh, faith, I don't want to eat with my betters – not I.' And she continued firm in her resolution, and ate apart.

The vegetables had been well cooked over a wood fire – the only way to cook a vegetable properly – and the bacon was well-boiled. The curate ate heartily: he thought he had never tasted such potatoes and cabbage in his life, which he probably had not, for they had been just brought in from the garden, so that the very freshness of the morning was still in them. When he had finished he asked her how much he owed for the repast, which he had much enjoyed.

'Oh, I don't want to be paid for that bit of snack 'a b'lieve!'

'But really you must take something. It was an excellent meal.'

''Tis all my own growing, that's true. But I don't take money for a bit o' victuals. I've never done such a thing in my life.'

'I should feel much happier if you would.'

She seemed unsettled by his feeling, and added as by compulsion, 'Well, then; I suppose twopence won't hurt ye?'

'Twopence?'

'Yes. Twopence.'

'Why, my good woman, that's no charge at all. I am sure it worth this, at least.' And he laid down a shilling.

'I tell 'ee 'tis twopence, and no more!' she said firmly. 'Why, bless the man, it didn't cost me more than three halfpence, and that leaves me a fair quarter profit. The bacon is the heaviest item; that may perhaps be a penny. The taters I've got plenty of, and the cabbage is going to waste.'

He thereupon argued no further, paid the limited sum demanded, and went to the door. 'And where does that road lead?' he asked, by way of engaging her in a little friendly conversation before parting, and pointing to a white lane which branched from the direct highway near her door.

'They tell me that it leads to Enckworth.'

'And how far is Enckworth?'

'Three mile, they say. But God knows if 'tis true.'

'You haven't lived here long, then?'

'Five-and-thirty year come Martinmas.'

'And yet you have never been to Enckworth?'

'Not I. Why should I ever have been to Enckworth? I never had any business there – a great mansion of a place, holding people that I've no more doings with than with the people of the moon. No: there's on'y two places I ever go to from year's end to year's end: that's once a fortnight to Anglebury, to do my bit o' marketing; and once a week to my parish church.'

'Which is that?'

'Why, Kingscreech.'

'Oh – then you are in my parish?'

'Maybe. Just on the outskirts.'

'I didn't know the parish extended so far. I'm a new comer. Well, I hope we may meet again. Good afternoon to you.'

When the curate was next talking to his rector he casually observed: 'By the way, that's a curious old soul who lives out towards Corvsgate – old Mrs – I don't know her name – a deaf old woman.'

'You mean old Mrs Chundle, I suppose.'

'She tells me she's lived there five-and-thirty years, and has never been to Enckworth, three miles off. She goes to two places only, from year's end to year's end – to the market town, and to church on Sundays.'

'To church on Sundays. H'm. She rather exaggerates her travels, to my thinking. I've been rector here thirteen years, and I have certainly never seen her at church in my time.'

'A wicked old woman. What can she think of herself for such deception!'

'She didn't know you belonged here when she said it, and could find out the untruth of her story. I warrant she wouldn't have said it to me!' And the rector chuckled.

On reflection the curate felt that this was decidedly a case for his ministrations, and on the first spare morning he strode across to the cottage beyond the ruin. He found its occupant of course at home.

'Drawing picters again?' she asked, looking up from the hearth, where she was scouring the fire-dogs.

'No. I come on more important matters, Mrs Chundle. I am the new curate of this parish.'

'You said you was last time. And after you had told me and went away I said to myself, he'll be here again sure enough, hang me if I didn't. And here you be.'

'Yes. I hope you don't mind?'

'Oh, no. You find us a roughish lot, I make no doubt?'

'Well, I won't go into that. But I think it was a very culpable – unkind thing of you to tell me you came to church every Sunday, when I find you've not been seen there for years.'

'Oh – did I tell 'ee that?'

'You certainly did.'

'Now I wonder what I did that for?'

'I wonder too.'

'Well you could ha' guessed, after all, that I didn't come to any service. Lord, what's the good o' my lumpering all the way to church and back again, when I'm as deaf as a plock? Your own commonsense ought to have told 'ee that 'twas but a figure o' speech, seeing you was a pa'son.'

'Don't you think you could hear the service if you were to sit close to the reading-desk and pulpit?'

'I'm sure I couldn't. O no – not a word. Why I couldn't hear anything even at that time when Isaac Coggs used to cry the Amens out loud beyond anything that's done nowadays, and they had the barrel-organ for the tunes–years and years agone, when I was stronger in my narves than now.'

'H'm – I'm sorry. There's one thing I could do, which I would with pleasure, if you'll use it. I could get you an ear-trumpet. Will you use it?'

'Ay, sure. That I woll. I don't care what I use–'tis all the same to me.'

'And you'll come?'

'Yes. I may as well go there as bide here, I suppose.'

The ear-trumpet was purchased by the zealous young man, and the next Sunday, to the great surprise of the parishioners when they arrived, Mrs Chundle was discovered in the front seat of the nave of Kingscreech Church, facing the rest of the congregation with an unmoved countenance.

She was the centre of observation through the whole morning service. The trumpet, elevated at a high angle, shone and flashed in the sitters' eyes as the chief object in the sacred edifice.

The curate could not speak to her that morning, and called the next day to inquire the result of the experiment. As soon as she saw him in the distance she began shaking her head.

'No, no,' she said decisively as he approached. 'I knowed 'twas all nonsense.'

'What?'

'Twasn't a mossel o' good, and so I could have told 'ee before. A wasting your money in jimcracks upon a' old 'ooman like me.'

'You couldn't hear? Dear me – how disappointing.'

'You might as well have been mouthing at me from the top o' Creech Barrow.'

'That's unfortunate.'

'I shall never come no more – never – to be made such a fool of as that again.'

The curate mused. 'I'll tell you what, Mrs Chundle. There's one thing more to try, and only one. If that fails I suppose we shall have to give it up. It is a plan I have heard of, though I have never myself tried it; it's having a sound-tube fixed, with its lower mouth in the seat immediately below the pulpit, where you would sit, the tube running up inside the pulpit with its upper end opening in a bell-mouth just beside the book-board. The voice of the preacher enters the bell-mouth, and is carried down directly to the listener's ear. Do you understand?'

'Exactly.'

'And you'll come, if I put it up at my own expense?'

'Ay, I suppose. I'll try it, e'en though I said I wouldn't. I may as well do that as do nothing, I reckon.'

The kind-hearted curate, at great trouble to himself, obtained the tube and had it fixed vertically as described, the upper mouth being immediately under the face of whoever should preach, and on the following Sunday morning it was to be tried. As soon as he came from the vestry the curate perceived to his satisfaction Mrs Chundle in the seat beneath, erect and at attention, her head close to the lower orifice of the sound-pipe, and a look of great complacency that her soul required a special machinery to save it, while other people's could be saved in a commonplace way. The rector read the prayers from the desk on the opposite side, which part of the service Mrs Chundle could follow easily enough by the help of the prayer-book; and in due course the curate mounted the eight steps into the wooden octagon, gave out his text, and began to deliver his discourse.

It was a fine frosty morning in early winter, and he had not got far with his sermon when he became conscious of a steam rising from the bell-mouth of the tube, obviously caused by Mrs Chundle's breathing at the lower end, and it was accompanied by a suggestion of onion-stew. However he preached on awhile, hoping it would cease, holding in his left hand his finest cambric handkerchief kept especially for Sunday morning services. At length, no longer able to endure the odour, he lightly dropped the handkerchief into the bell of the tube, without stopping for a moment the eloquent flow of his words; and he had the satisfaction of feeling himself in comparatively pure air.

He heard a fidgeting below; and presently there arose to him over the pulpit-edge a hoarse whisper: 'The pipe's chokt!'

'Now, as you will perceive, my brethren,' continued the curate, unheeding the interruption; 'by applying this test to ourselves, our discernment of – '

'The pipe's chokt!' came up in a whisper yet louder and hoarser.

'Our discernment of actions as morally good, or indifferent, will be much quickened, and we shall be materially helped in our – '

Suddenly came a violent puff of warm wind, and he beheld his handkerchief rising from the bell of the tube and floating to the pulpit-floor. The little boys in the gallery laughed, thinking it a miracle. Mrs Chundle had, in fact, applied her mouth to the bottom end, blown with all her might, and cleared the tube. In a few seconds the atmosphere of the pulpit became as before, to the curate's great discomfiture. Yet stop the orifice again he dared not, lest the old woman should make a still greater disturbance and draw the attention of the congregation to this unseemly situation.

'If you carefully analyse the passage I have quoted,' he continued in somewhat uncomfortable accents, 'you will perceive that it naturally suggests three points for consideration – '

('It's not onions: it's peppermint,' he said to himself.)

'Namely, mankind in its unregenerate state – '

('And cider.')

'The incidence of the law, and loving-kindness or grace, which we will now severally consider – '

('And pickled cabbage. What a terrible supper she must have made!')

'Under the twofold aspect of external and internal consciousness.'

Thus the reverend gentleman continued strenuously for perhaps five minutes longer: then he could stand it no more. Desperately thrusting his thumb into the hole he drew the threads of his distracted discourse together, the while hearing her blow vigorously to dislodge the plug. But he stuck to the hole, and brought his sermon to a premature close.

He did not call on Mrs Chundle the next week, a slight cooling of his zeal for her spiritual welfare being manifest; but he encountered her at the house of another cottager whom he was visiting; and she immediately addressed him as a partner in the same enterprize.

'I could hear beautiful!' she said. 'Yes; every word! Never did I know such a wonderful machine as that there pipe. But you forgot what you was doing once or twice, and put your handkercher on the top o' en, and stopped the sound a bit. Please not to do that again, for it makes me lose a lot. Howsomever, I shall come every Sunday morning reg'lar now, please God.'

The curate quivered internally.

'And will ye come to my house once in a while and read to me?'

'Of course.'

Surely enough the next Sunday the ordeal was repeated for him. In the evening he told his trouble to the rector. The rector chuckled.

'You've brought it upon yourself' he said. 'You don't know this parish so well as I. You should have left the old woman alone.'

'I suppose I should?!'

'Thank Heaven, she thinks nothing of my sermons, and doesn't come when I preach. Ha, ha!'

'Well,' said the curate somewhat ruffled, 'I must do something. I cannot stand this. I shall tell her not to come.'

'You can hardly do that.'

'And I've half-promised to go and read to her. But – I shan't go.'

'She's probably forgotten by this time that you promised.'

A vision of his next Sunday in the pulpit loomed horridly before the young man, and at length he determined to escape the experience. The pipe should be taken down. The next morning he gave directions, and the removal was carried out.

A day or two later a message arrived from her, saying that she wished to see him. Anticipating a terrific attack from the irate old woman he put off going to her for a day, and when he trudged out towards her house on the following afternoon it was in a vexed mood. Delicately nurtured man as he was he had determined not to re-erect the tube, and hoped he might hit on some new modus vivendi, even if at any inconvenience to Mrs Chundle, in a situation that had become intolerable as it was last week.

'Thank Heaven, the tube is gone,' he said to himself as he walked; 'and nothing will make me put it up again!'

On coming near he saw to his surprise that the calico curtains of the cottage windows were all drawn. He went up to the door, which was ajar; and a little girl peeped through the opening.

'How is Mrs Chundle?' he asked blandly.

'She's dead, sir,' said the girl in a whisper.

'Dead?… Mrs Chundle dead?'

'Yes, sir.'

A woman now came. 'Yes, 'tis so, sir. She went off quite sudden-like about two hours ago. Well, you see, sir, she was over seventy years of age, and last Sunday she was rather late in starting for church, having to put her bit o' dinner ready before going out; and was very anxious to be in time. So she hurried overmuch, and runned up the hill, which at her time of life she ought not to have done. It upset her heart, and she's been poorly all the week since, and that made her send for 'ee. Two or three times she said she hoped you would come soon, as you'd promised to, and you were so staunch and faithful in wishing to do her good, that she knew 'twas not by your own wish you didn't arrive. But she would not let us send again, as it might trouble 'ee too much, and there might be other poor folks needing you. She worried to think she might not be able to listen to 'ee next Sunday, and feared you'd be hurt at it, and think her remiss. But she was eager to hear you again later on. However, 'twas ordained otherwise for the poor soul, and she was soon gone. 'I've found a real friend at last,' she said. 'He's a man in a thousand. He's not ashamed of a' old woman, and he holds that her soul is worth saving as well as richer people's. She said I was to give you this.'

It was a small folded piece of paper, directed to him and sealed with a thimble. On opening it he found it to be what she called her will, in which she had left him her bureau, caseclock, settle, four-post bedstead, and framed sampler – in fact all the furniture of any account that she possessed.

The curate went out, like Peter at the cock-crow. He was a meek young man, and as he went his eyes were wet. When he reached a lonely place in the lane he stood still thinking, and kneeling down in the dust of the road rested his elbow in one hand and covered his face with the other. Thus he remained some minutes or so, a black shape on the hot white of the sunned trackway; till he rose, brushed the knees of his trousers, and walked on.

ONE OF THESE DAYS

GABRIEL GARCIA MARQUEZ

Gabriel Garcia Marquez (1927-2014), winner of many prizes, was Columbia's most famous writer. He is best known for a writing style called 'Magic Realism' which, as its name suggests, blends the magical with the realistic. However, 'One of These Days' is a straightforwardly realistic story. It was published in 1962, shortly after a period known as 'La Violencia', when civil war between conservatives and liberals resulted in the deaths of at least 200,000 Colombians

Marquez often wrote about politics and political violence, both as a journalist and in his fiction. He was particularly concerned with the way ordinary, and especially poor, people have been affected.

Monday dawned warm and rainless. Aurelio Escovar, a dentist without a degree, and a very early riser, opened his office at six. He took some false teeth, still mounted in their plaster mould, out of the glass case and put on the table a fistful of instruments which he arranged in size order, as if they were on display. He wore a collarless striped shirt, closed at the neck with a golden stud, and pants held up with suspenders. He was erect and skinny, with a look that rarely corresponded to the situation, the way deaf people have of looking.

When he had things arranged on the table, he pulled the drill toward the dental chair and sat down to polish the false teeth. He seemed not to be thinking about what he was doing, but worked steadily, pumping the drill with his feet, even when he didn't need it.

After eight he stopped for a while to look at the sky through the window, and he saw two pensive buzzards who were drying themselves in the sun on the ridgepole of the house next door. He went on working with the idea that before lunch it would rain again. The shrill voice of his eleven-year-old son interrupted his concentration.

'Papa.'

'What?'

'The Mayor wants to know if you'll pull his tooth.'

'Tell him I'm not here.'

He was polishing a gold tooth. He held it at arm's length, and examined it with his eyes half closed. His son shouted again from the little waiting room.

'He says you are, too, because he can hear you.'

The dentist kept examining the tooth. Only when he had put it on the table with the finished work did he say:

'So much the better.'

He operated the drill again. He took several pieces of a bridge out of a cardboard box where he kept the things he still had to do and began to polish the gold.

'Papa.'

'What?'

He still hadn't changed his expression.

'He says if you don't take out his tooth, he'll shoot you.'

Without hurrying, with an extremely tranquil movement, he stopped pedalling the drill, pushed it away from the chair, and pulled the lower drawer of the table all the way out. There was a revolver. 'O.K.,' he said. 'Tell him to come and shoot me.'

He rolled the chair over opposite the door, his hand resting on the edge of the drawer. The Mayor appeared at the door. He had shaved the left side of his face, but the other side, swollen and in pain, had a five-day-old beard. The dentist saw many nights of desperation in his dull eyes. He closed the drawer with his fingertips and said softly:

'Sit down.'

'Good morning,' said the Mayor.

'Morning,' said the dentist.

While the instruments were boiling, the Mayor leaned his skull on the headrest of the chair and felt better. His breath was icy. It was a poor office: an old wooden chair, the pedal drill, a glass case with ceramic bottles. Opposite the chair was a window with a shoulder-high cloth curtain. When he felt the dentist approach, the Mayor braced his heels and opened his mouth.

Aurelo Escovar turned his head toward the light. After inspecting the infected tooth, he closed the Mayor's jaw with a cautious pressure of his fingers.

'It has to be without anaesthesia,' he said.

'Why?'

'Because you have an abscess.'

The Mayor looked him in the eye. 'All right,' he said, and tried to smile. The dentist did not return the smile. He brought the basin of sterilised instruments to the worktable and took them out of the water with a pair of cold tweezers, still without hurrying. Then he pushed the spittoon with the tip of his shoe, and went to wash his hands in the washbasin. He did all this without looking at the Mayor. But the Mayor didn't take his eyes off him.

It was a lower wisdom tooth. The dentist spread his feet and grasped the tooth with the hot forceps. The Mayor seized the arms of the chair, braced his feet with all his strength, and felt an icy void in his kidneys, but didn't make a sound. The dentist moved only his wrist. Without rancour, rather with a bitter tenderness, he said:

'Now you'll pay for our twenty dead men.'

The Mayor felt the crunch of bones in his jaw, and his eyes filled with tears. But he didn't breathe until he felt the tooth come out. Then he saw it through his tears. It seemed so foreign to his pain that he failed to understand his torture of the five previous nights.

Bent over the spittoon, sweating, panting, he unbuttoned his tunic and reached for the handkerchief in his pants pocket. The dentist gave him a clean cloth.

'Dry your tears,' he said.

The Mayor did. He was trembling. While the dentist washed his hands, he saw the crumbling ceiling and a dusty spider web with spider's eggs and dead insects. The dentist returned, drying his hands. 'Go to bed,' he said, 'and gargle with salt water.' The Mayor stood up, said goodbye with a casual military salute, and walked toward the door, stretching his legs, without buttoning up his tunic.

'Send the bill,' he said.

'To you or the town?'

The Mayor didn't look at him. He closed the door and said though the screen:

'It's the same damn thing.'

THE RETURN

NGUGI WA THIONG'O

Ngugi Wa Thiong'o (1938-) is a Kenyan writer, well known for his novels, short stories and non-fiction, and also his political activism. He has spent time in prison for his campaigning against oppressive Kenyan regimes in the past, something he might well have drawn on for 'The Return', first published in 1965.

Ngugi originally wrote in English, but switched to writing in his native Gikuyu because he wanted to promote and value his own language and identity.

The road was long. Whenever he took a step forward, little clouds of dust rose, whirled angrily behind him, and then slowly settled again. But a thin train of dust was left in the air, moving like smoke. He walked on, however, unmindful of the dust and ground under his feet. Yet with every step he seemed more and more conscious of the hardness and apparent animosity of the road. Not that he looked down; on the contrary, he looked straight ahead as if he would, any time now, see a familiar object that would hail him as a friend and tell him that he was near home. But the road stretched on.

He made quick, springing steps, his left hand dangling freely by the side of his once white coat, now torn and worn out. His right hand, bent at the elbow, held on to a string tied to a small bundle on his slightly drooping back. The bundle, well wrapped with a cotton cloth that had once been covered with printed red flowers now faded out, swung from side to side in harmony with the rhythm of his steps. The bundle held the bitterness and hardships of the years spent in detention camps. Now and then, he looked at the sun on its homeward journey. Sometimes he darted quick side-

Literary Shorts – An Anthology   © English & Media Centre, 2014

glances at the small hedged strips of land which, with their sickly-looking crops, maize, beans and peas, appeared much as everything else did – unfriendly. The whole country was dull and seemed weary. To Kamau, this was nothing new. He remembered that, even before the *Mau Mau emergency*, the over-tilled *Gikuyu* holdings wore haggard looks, in contrast to the sprawling green fields in the settled *area*.

A path branched to the left. He hesitated for a moment and then made up his mind. For the first time, his eyes brightened a little as he went along the path that would take him down the valley and then to the village. At last home was near and, with that realisation, that far-away look of the weary traveller seemed to desert him for a while.

The valley and the vegetation along it were in deep contrast to the surrounding country. For here, green bush and trees thrived. This could only mean one thing: Honia River still flowed. He quickened his steps as if he could scarcely believe this to be true till he had actually set his eyes on the river. It was there; it still flowed. Honia, where so often he had bathed, plunging stark naked into its cool living water, warmed his heart as he watched its serpentine movement round the rocks and heard its slight murmurs. A painful exhilaration passed through him, and for a moment he longed for those days. He sighed. Perhaps the river would not recognise in his hardened features that same boy to whom the riverside world had meant everything. Yet as he approached Honia, he felt more akin to it than he had felt to anything else since his release.

A group of women were drawing water. He was excited, for he could recognize one or two from his Ridge. There was the middle-aged Wanjiku, whose deaf son had been killed by the Security Forces just before he himself was arrested. She had always been a darling of the village, having a smile for everyone and food for all. Would they receive him? Would they give him a hero's welcome? He thought so. Had he not always been a favourite all along the Ridge? And had he not fought for the land? He wanted to run and shout: 'Here I am. I have come back to you.' But he desisted. He was a man.

'Is it well with you?' A few voices responded.

The other women, with tired and worn features, looked at him mutely as if his greeting was of no consequence. Why! Had he been so long in the camp? His spirits were dampened as he feebly asked: 'Do you not remember me?' Again they looked at him. They stared at him with cold, hard looks; like everything else, they seemed to be deliberately refusing to know or own him.

It was Wanjiku who at last recognised him. But there was neither warmth nor enthusiasm in her voice as she said, 'Oh, is it you, Kamau? We thought you –' She did not continue. Only now he noticed something else – surprise? fear? He could not tell. He saw their quick glances dart at him and he knew for certain that a secret, from which he was excluded, bound them together.

'Perhaps I am no longer one of them!' he bitterly reflected. But they told him of the new village. The old village of scattered huts spread thinly over the Ridge was no more.

He left them, feeling embittered and cheated. The old village had not even waited for him. And suddenly he felt a strong nostalgia for his old home, friends and surroundings. He thought of his father, mother and – and – he dared not think about her. But for all that, Muthoni, just as she had been in the old days, came back to his mind. His heart beat faster. He felt desire, and a warmth thrilled through him. He quickened his step. He forgot the village women as he remembered his wife. He had stayed with her for a mere two weeks; then he had been swept away by the Colonial Forces. Like many others, he had been hurriedly screened and then taken to detention without trial. And all that time he had thought of nothing but the village and his beautiful woman.

The others had been like him. They had talked of nothing but their homes. One day he was working next to another detainee from Muranga. Suddenly the detainee, Njoroge, stopped breaking stones. He sighed heavily. His worn-out eyes had a far-away look.

'What's wrong, man? What's the matter with you?' Kamau asked.

'It is my wife. I left her expecting a baby. I have no idea what has happened to her.'

Another detainee put in: 'As for me, I left my woman with a baby. She had just been delivered. We were all happy. But on the same day I was arrested...'

And so they went on. All of them longed for one day – the day of their return home. Then life would begin anew.

Kamau himself had left his wife without a child. He had not even finished paying the bride-price. But now he would go, seek work in Nairobi and pay off the remainder to Muthoni's parents. Life would indeed begin anew. They would have a son and bring him up in their own home. With these prospects before his eyes, he quickened his steps. He wanted to run – no, fly, to hasten his return. He was now nearing the top of the hill. He wished he could suddenly meet his brothers and sisters. Would they ask him questions? He would, at any rate, not tell them everything that had happened: the beating, the screening and the work on the roads and in quarries with an *askari* always nearby ready to kick him if he relaxed. Yes. He had suffered many humiliations, and he had not resisted. Was there any need? But his soul and all the vigour of his manhood had rebelled and bled with rage and bitterness.

One day these *wazungu* would go!

One day his people would be free! Then, then – he did not know what he would do. However, he bitterly assured himself, no one would ever flout his manhood again.

He mounted the hill and then stopped. The whole plain lay below. The new village was before him – rows and rows of compact mud huts, crouching on the plain under the fast-vanishing sun. Dark blue smoke curled upwards from various huts, to form a dark mist that hovered over the village. Beyond, the deep, blood-red sinking sun sent out finger-like streaks of light that thinned outwards and mingled with the grey mist shrouding the distant hills.

In the village, he moved from street to street, meeting new faces. He inquired. He found his home. He stopped at the entrance to the yard and breathed hard and full. This was the moment of his return home. His father sat huddled up on a three-legged stool. He was now very aged and Kamau pitied the old man. But he had been spared – yes, spared to see his son's return.

'Father!'

The old man did not answer. He just looked at Kamau with strange vacant eyes. Kamau was impatient. He felt annoyed and irritated. Did he not see him? Would he behave like the women Kamau had met at the river?

In the street, naked and half-naked children were playing, throwing dust at one another. The sun had already set and it looked as if there would be moonlight.

'Father, don't you remember me?' Hope was shrinking in him. He felt tired. Then he saw his father suddenly start and tremble like a leaf. He saw him stare with unbelieving eyes. Fear was discernible in those eyes. His mother came, and his brothers too. They crowded around him. His aged mother clung to him and sobbed hard.

'I knew my son would come. I knew he was not dead.'

'Why, who told you I was dead?'

'That Karanja, son of Njogu.'

And then Kamau understood. He understood his trembling father. He understood the women at the river. But one thing puzzled him: he had never been in the same detention camp with Karanja. Anyway he had come back. He wanted now to see Muthoni. Why had she not come out? He wanted to shout, 'I have come, Muthoni; I am here.' He looked around. His mother understood him. She quickly darted a glance at her man and then simply said: 'Muthoni went away.'

Kamau felt something cold settle in his stomach. He looked at the village huts and the dullness of the land. He wanted to ask some questions but he dared not. He could not yet believe that Muthoni had gone. But he knew by the look of the women at the river, by the look of his parents, that she was gone.

'She was a good daughter to us,' his mother was explaining. 'She waited for you and patiently bore all the ills of the land. Then Karanja came and said that you were dead. Your father believed him. She believed him too and mourned for a month. Karanja constantly paid us visits. He was of your *rika*, you know. Then she got a child. We could have kept her. But where is the land? Where is the food? With land consolidation, our last security was taken away. We let Karanja go with her. Other women have done worse – gone to town. Only the infirm and the old have remained here.'

He was not listening; the coldness in his stomach slowly changed to bitterness. He felt bitter against all, all the people including his father and mother. They had betrayed him. They had leagued against him, and

Literary Shorts – An Anthology   © English & Media Centre, 2014

Karanja had always been his rival. Five years admittedly was not a short time. But why did she go? Why did they allow her to go? He wanted to speak. Yes, speak and denounce everything – the women at the river, the village and the people who dwelt there. But he could not. This bitter thing was choking him.

'You – you gave my own away?' he whispered.

'Listen, child, child…'

The big yellow moon dominated the horizon. He hurried away bitter and blind, and only stopped when he came to the Honia River.

And standing on the bank, he saw not the river, but instead his hopes dashed to the ground. The river moved swiftly, making ceaseless monotonous murmurs. In the forest the crickets and other insects kept up an incessant buzz. And above, the moon shone bright. He tried to remove his coat, and the small bundle he had held on to so firmly fell. It rolled down the bank and, before Kamau knew what was happening, it was floating swiftly down the river. For a time he was shocked and wanted to retrieve it. What would he show his – Oh, had he forgotten so soon? His wife had gone. And the little things that had so strangely reminded him of her, and that he had guarded all those years, had gone! He did not know why, but somehow he felt relieved. Thoughts of drowning himself dispersed. He began to put on his coat, murmuring to himself, 'Why should she have waited for me? Why should all the changes have waited for my return?'

THE WHITE TROUSERS

YAŞAR KEMAL

> **Yaşar Kemal** (1923-) is a Turkish writer. He had a difficult start in life, losing his right eye in an accident with a knife and witnessing his father being stabbed to death. His mother's family were bandits. Even when he was still at school he was known as a folk singer and a poet, and as he grew up, he became interested in writing for a living. At first he worked as a letter writer, then as a journalist, before becoming a novelist.
>
> He usually sets his fiction in Anatolia, the region of Turkey in which he grew up. Not surprisingly, given his difficult start in life, he often writes about those who are struggling to make their way in life, and people getting revenge.
>
> 'The White Trousers' was first published in 1968.

It was hot. The boy Mustafa held the shoe listlessly and gazed out of the shop at the sun-impacted street with its uneven cobbles. He felt he would never be able to mend this shoe. It was the most tattered thing he had ever come across. He looked up tentatively, but the cobbler was bent over his work. He placed the shoe on the bench and hammered in a nail haphazardly.

'I can't do it,' he murmured at last.

'What's that, Mustafa?' said the cobbler, raising his head for a moment. 'Why, you haven't begun to try yet!'

'But, Master,' protested the boy, 'it comes apart as soon as I put in a stitch...'

The cobbler was silent.

Mustafa tackled the shoe again. His face was running with sweat and the sun had dropped nearer the distant hills when Hassan Bey, a well-to-do friend of the cobbler's, stepped into the shop.

'My friend,' he said, 'I need a boy to help fire my brick-kiln. Will you let me have this one? Only for three days.'

'Would you work at the brick-kiln, Mustafa?' asked the cobbler. 'It's for three days and three nights too, you know...'

'The pay is one and a half liras a day,' said Hassan Bey.

'All you'll have to do is give a hand to Jumali. You know Jumali who lives down by the river? He's a good man, won't let you work yourself out.'

Mustafa's black eyes shone.

'All right, Uncle Hassan,' he said. 'But I'll have to ask Mother...'

'Well, ask her, and be at my orange grove tomorrow. The kiln's in the field next to it. You'll start work in the afternoon. I won't be there, but you'll find Jumali.'

The cobbler paid him twenty-five kurush a week. A whole month and only one lira! It was July already, and a pair of summer shoes cost two liras, a pair of white trousers three... But now, four and a half liras would be his for only three days' work! What a stroke of luck!... First you wash your hands, but properly, with soap... Then you unwrap the white canvas shoes... Your socks must be white too. You must be careful, very careful with the white trousers. They get soiled so quickly. Your fingers should hardly touch them. And so to the bridge where the girls stroll in the cool of the evening, the breeze swelling their skirts... The breeze tautening the white trousers against your legs...

'Mother!' he cried, bursting into the house. 'I'm going to fire Hassan Bey's brick-kiln with Jumali!'

'Who says so? Certainly not!'

'But, Mother...'

'My child, you don't know what firing a kiln means. Can you go without sleep for three days and three nights? God knows I have trouble enough waking you up in the morning!'

'But, Mother, this is different...'

'You'll fall asleep, I tell you. You'll never stand it.'

'Look, Mother, you know Sami, Tewfik Bey's son Sami?' he said hopefully.

'Well?'

'Those white trousers of his and the white shoes? Snow-white! I've got a silk shirt in the trunk. I'll wear that too. Wouldn't I look well?'

Mustafa knew his mother. The tears rose to her eyes. She bowed her head.

'Wouldn't I, Mother? Now, wouldn't I?'

'My darling, you'd look well in anything...'

'Vayis the tailor'll do it for me. Mother dear, say I can go!'

'Well, I don't know...' she said doubtfully.

He saw she was giving in and flung himself on her neck.

'When I'm big...' he began.

'You'll work very hard.'

'And then?' he prompted.

'You'll make a beautiful orange grove of that empty field of ours near the stream. You'll have a horse of your own to ride... You'll order navy blue suits from tailors in Adana...'

'And then?'

'Then you'll tile the roof of our house so it won't let in the rain.'

'Then?'

'You'll be just like your father.'

'And if my father hadn't died?'

'You'd have gone to school and studied and become a great man...'

'But now?'

'If your Father had been alive...'

'Look,' said Mustafa, 'I'll have a gold watch when I'm big, won't I?'

***

The next morning he was up and away before sunrise. The dust on the road felt cool and soft under his bare feet. A flood of light was surging up behind the hill. When he came to the kiln, the sun was sitting on the crest like a great round ember. He bent over to the mouth of the kiln. It was dark inside. Around it brushwood had been heaped in little hillocks.

It was almost noon when Jumali arrived. He was a big man who walked ponderously, picking his way. Ignoring Mustafa, he stopped before the kiln and thrust his head inside. Then he turned back.

'What're you doing around here, hey?' he barked.

The boy was struck with fear. He felt like taking to his heels.

'What're you standing there stuck for, hey?' shouted Jumali.

'Hassan Bey sent me,' stammered Mustafa. 'To help you...'

With surprising agility Jumali swung his heavy frame impatiently back to the kiln.

'Now that's fine!' he growled. 'What does Hassan Bey think he's doing, sending along a child not bigger than the palm of your hand?' He flung his hand out. 'Not bigger than this hand! You go right back and tell him to find someone else.'

Mustafa was dumb with dismay. He took a few wavering steps towards the town. Then he stopped. The white trousers danced before his eyes. He wanted to cry.

'Uncle Jumali,' he begged weakly, 'I'll work harder than a grown man...'

'Listen to the pup! Do you know what it means to fire a kiln?'

'Oh yes...'

'Why, you little bastard, three days, three nights of feeding wood into this hole you see here, taking it in turns, you and I...'

'I know, I know!'

'Listen to the little bastard! Did you learn all this in your mother's womb? Now bugger off and stop pestering me.'

Mustafa had a flash of inspiration.

'I can't go back,' he said. 'Hassan Bey paid me in advance and I've already spent the money.'

'Go away!' shouted Jumali. 'You'll get me into trouble.'

Mustafa rebelled.

'But why? Why d'you want to take the bread out of my mouth? Just because I'm a child... I can work as hard as anyone.' Suddenly he ran up to Jumali and grasped his hand. 'I swear it, Uncle Jumali! You'll see how I'll feed that kiln. Anyway, I've spent the pay...'

'Well, all right,' Jumali said at last. 'We'll see...'

He lit a stick of pinewood and thrust it in. The wood crackled and a long tongue of flame spurted out.

'Damn!' he cursed. 'Filled it up to bursting, they have, the bastards! Everything they do is wrong.'

Still cursing, he gave Mustafa a few instructions. Then he lit a cigarette and moved off into the shade of a fig-tree.

When the flames that were lapping the mouth of the kiln had receded, Mustafa picked up an armful of brushwood and threw it in. Then another... And another...

The dusty road, the thick-spreading fig-trees, the stream that flowed like molten tin, the ashen sky, the lone bird flapping by, the scorched grass, the small wilting yellow flowers, the whole world drooped wearily under the impact of the noonday heat. Mustafa's face was as red as the flames, his shirt dripping, as he ran carrying the brushwood from the heat of the sun to the heat of the kiln.

At the close of the sizzling afternoon, little white clouds rise up in clusters far off in the south over the Mediterranean, heralding the cool moist breeze that will soon enwrap the heat-baked creatures as in a wet soothing towel. As the first fresh puff of wind stirred up the dust on the road, Jumali called to Mustafa from where he lay supine in the heavy shade of the fig-tree.

'Hey, boy, come along and let's eat!'

Mustafa was quivering with exhaustion and hunger.

Hassan Bey had provided Jumali with a bundle of food. There was white cheese, green onions and wafer-bread. They fell to without a word. The sun sank down behind the poplar trees that stood out like a dark curtain against the glow. Mustafa picked up the jug and went to the stream. The water tasted like warm blood. They drank it thirstily. Jumali wiped his long moustache with the back of his hand.

'I'm going to sleep a while, Mustafa,' he said. 'Wake me up when you're tired, eh?'

It was long past midnight. The moon had dropped behind the wall of poplars. Mustafa's thin sweating face shone red in the blaze. He threw in an armful of wood and watched the wild onrush of flames swallow it up. There was a loud crackling at first, then a long, long moaning sound that was almost human.

Like a baby crying its heart out, he thought.

'Are you tired? D'you want me?' came Jumali's sleepy voice.

A tremor shook his body. He felt a cold sweat breaking out all over him.

'Oh no, Uncle Jumali!' he cried. 'I never get tired. You go on sleeping.'

***

He could not bear to go near the kiln any more. Now he heaped as much wood as possible close to the opening and shoved it in with the long wooden fork. Then, backing before the sudden surge of heat, he scrambled on to a mound near by and stood awhile against the night breeze. But the air bore down, heavy and stifling, drowning him.

There is a bird that sings just before the break of dawn. A very tiny bird. Its call is long-drawn and piercing. He heard the bird's call and saw a widening ribbon of light brighten up the sky behind the hill.

Just then Jumali woke up.

'Are you tired?' he asked.

'No... No... I'm not tired...' But his voice broke, strangling with tears.

Jumali rose and stretched himself.

'Go and sleep a little now,' he said.

He was asleep when Hassan Bey arrived.

'How's the boy doing?' he asked. 'Working all right?'

Jumali's lips curled.

'A chit of a child…' he said.

'Well, you'll have to shift along as best you can. I'll make it worth your while,' said Hassan Bey as he left.

When Mustafa awoke the sun was heaving down upon him and the earth was like red-hot iron. His bones ached as though they had been pounded in a mortar. Setting his teeth, he struggled up and ran to the kiln.

'Uncle Jumali,' he faltered, 'I'm sorry I slept so long…'

'I told you you'd never make it,' said Jumali sourly.

Mustafa did not answer. He scraped up some brushwood and began feeding the kiln. After a while he felt a little better.

Hurray! he thought. We've weathered the first day.

But the two huge searing days loomed before him and the stifling clamminess of the infernal nights. He chased the thought away and conjured up the image of the white trousers…

***

The last night… The moon bright over the poplar trees…

'Wake me up if you get tired,' says Jumali…

The fire has to be kept up at the same level or the bricks will not bake and a whole two days' work will have been in vain. The flames must flare out greedily licking at the night. The hated flames… He has not the strength to reach the refreshing mound any longer. He can only throw himself on the ground and let the moist coolness of the earth seep into his body. But always the fear in his heart that sleep will overcome him…

His eyes were clinging to the east, groping for the ribbon of light. But it was pitch dark and Jumali snored on loudly.

Damn you, Uncle Jumali! Damn you…

Suddenly, the whole world started trembling. The dark curtain of poplars, the hills, the flames, the kiln were turning round and round. He was going to vomit.

'Jumali! Uncle Jumali...'

He had fainted.

It was a good while before Jumali called again in his drowsy voice.

'Are you tired, Mustafa?'

There was no answer. Then he caught sight of the darkened kiln. He rushed up and fetched the child a furious kick.

'You've done for me, you little bastard! They'll make me pay for the bricks now...'

He peered into the opening and took hope. A few small flames were still wavering against the inner wall.

Mustafa came to as the dawn was breaking. His heart quaked at the sight of Jumali, his hairy chest bared, stoking the kiln.

'Uncle Jumali,' he faltered, 'really, I never meant to...'

Jumali cast an angry glance over his shoulder.

'Shut up, damn you! Go to hell!'

Mustafa hung his head and sat there motionless until the sun rose over the hill. Then he fell asleep in the same position.

A brick kiln is large and spacious, rather like a well that has been capped with a dome. When it is first set alight the bricks take on a leaden hue. The second day, they turn a dull black. But on the morning of the third day, they are a fiery red...

Mustafa awoke with fear in his heart. The sun was quarter high and Hassan Bey was standing near the kiln. The bricks were sparkling like red crystal.

'Well, my boy?' Hassan Bey laughed. 'So we came here to sleep, did we?'

'Uncle, I swear that every night...'

Jumali threw him a dour look. He dared not go on.

They sealed up the mouth of the kiln.

***

The cobbler had shaggy eyebrows and a beard. His back was slightly hunched. The shop, dusty and cobwebby, smelled of leather and rawhide.

A week had gone by and still no sign of Hassan Bey. Mustafa was eating his heart out with anxiety, but he said nothing. Then one day Hassan Bey happened to pass before the shop.

'Hey, Hassan!' the cobbler called. 'When are you going to pay the lad here?'

Hassan Bey hesitated. Then he took a one-lira note and two twenty-five kurush coins and placed them on the bench.

'Here you are,' he said.

The cobbler stared at the money.

'But that's only a lira and a half. The child worked three days...'

'Well, he slept all the time, so I paid his share to Jumali. This, I'm giving him simply out of consideration for you,' said Hassan Bey, turning to leave.

'Uncle, I swear that every night...' began Mustafa, but his voice stuck in his throat. He lowered his head.

There was a long, painful silence.

'Look, Mustafa,' said the cobbler at last, 'you're more than an apprentice now. You patch soles really well. From now on you'll get a lira a week for your work.'

Mustafa raised his head slowly. His eyes were shining through the tears.

'Take these five liras,' said the cobbler, 'and give them to the tailor Vayis with my compliments. Tell him to cut your white trousers out of the best material he's got. With the rest of the money you can buy your shoes. I'm taking this fellow's money, so you owe me only three and a half weeks' pay...'

Mustafa laughed with glee.

In those days the blue five-lira note carried the picture of a wolf, its tongue hanging out as it galloped swift as the wind.

THE FLOWERS

ALICE WALKER

> **Alice Walker** (1944-) is an American author and activist. She is most famous for writing *The Color Purple*, a novel which tells the story of a woman's struggle to survive in a culture that is both racist and sexist. Though very short, 'The Flowers', first published in 1973, has much in common with Walker's other work in terms of setting, character and themes.

It seemed to Myop as she skipped lightly from hen house to pigpen to smokehouse that the days had never been as beautiful as these. The air held a keenness that made her nose twitch. The harvesting of the corn and cotton, peanuts and squash, made each day a golden surprise that caused excited little tremors to run up her jaws.

Myop carried a short, knobby stick. She struck out at random at chickens she liked, and worked out the beat of a song on the fence around the pigpen. She felt light and good in the warm sun. She was ten, and nothing existed for her but her song, the stick clutched in her dark brown hand, and the tat-de-ta-ta-ta of accompaniment.

Turning her back on the rusty boards of her family's sharecropper cabin, Myop walked along the fence till it ran into the stream made by the spring. Around the spring, where the family got drinking water, silver ferns and wild-flowers grew. Along the shallow banks pigs rooted. Myop watched the tiny white bubbles disrupt the thin black scale of soil and the water that silently rose and slid away down the stream.

She had explored the woods behind the house many times. Often, in late autumn, her mother took her to gather nuts among the fallen leaves. Today she made her own path, bouncing this way and that way, vaguely keeping an eye out for snakes. She found, in addition to various common but pretty ferns and leaves, an armful of strange blue flowers with velvety ridges and a sweetsuds bush full of the brown, fragrant buds.

By twelve o'clock, her arms laden with sprigs of her findings, she was a mile or more from home. She had often been as far before, but the strangeness of the land made it not as pleasant as her usual haunts. It seemed gloomy in the little cove in which she found herself. The air was damp, the silence close and deep.

Myop began to circle back to the house, back to the peacefulness of the morning. It was then she stepped smack into his eyes. Her heel became lodged in the broken ridge between brow and nose, and she reached down quickly, unafraid, to free herself. It was only when she saw his naked grin that she gave a little yelp of surprise.

He had been a tall man. From feet to neck covered a long space. His head lay beside him. When she pushed back the leaves and layers of earth and debris Myop saw that he'd had large white teeth, all of them cracked or broken, long fingers, and very big bones. All his clothes had rotted away except some threads of blue denim from his overalls. The buckles of the overalls had turned green.

Myop gazed around the spot with interest. Very near where she'd stepped into the head was a wild pink rose. As she picked it to add to her bundle she noticed a raised mound, a ring, around the rose's root. It was the rotted remains of a noose, a bit of shredding plowline, now blending benignly into the soil. Around an overhanging limb of a great spreading oak clung another piece. Frayed, rotted, bleached, and frazzled – barely there – but spinning restlessly in the breeze. Myop laid down her flowers.

And the summer was over.

MRS SILLY

WILLIAM TREVOR

> **William Trevor** (1928-) is an Irish author, regarded as one of the best writers of short stories in the English language. Typically his stories focus on characters who struggle to have their voices heard in society, such as children, or the elderly. 'Mrs Silly', first published in 1975, is a good example of his work in its sympathetic treatment of a young boy and his mother.

Michael couldn't remember a time when his father had been there. There'd always been the flat where he and his mother lived, poky and cluttered even though his mother tried so. Every Saturday his father came to collect him. He remembered a blue car and then a greenish one. The latest one was white, an Alfa-Romeo.

Saturday with his father was the highlight of the week. Unlike his mother's flat, his father's house was spacious and nicely carpeted. There was Gillian, his father's wife, who never seemed in a hurry, who smiled and didn't waste time. Her smile was cool, which matched the way she dressed. Her voice was quiet and reliable: Michael couldn't imagine it ever becoming shrill or weepy or furious, or in any other way getting out of control. It was a nice voice, as nice as Gillian herself.

His father and Gillian had two little girls, twins of six, two years younger than Michael. They lived near Cranleigh, in a half-timbered house in pretty wooded countryside. On Saturday mornings the drive from London took over an hour, but Michael never minded and on the way back he usually fell asleep. There was a room in the house that his father and Gillian had made his own, which the twins weren't allowed to enter in his absence. He had his

Triang train circuit there, on a table that had been specially built into the wall for it.

It was in this house, one Saturday afternoon, that Michael's father brought up the subject of Elton Grange. 'You're nearly nine, you know,' his father said. 'It's high time, really, old chap.'

Elton Grange was a preparatory school in Wiltshire, which Michael's father had gone to himself. He'd mentioned it many times before and so had Michael's mother, but in Michael's mind it was a place that belonged to the distant future – with Radley, where his father had gone, also. He certainly knew that he wasn't going to stay at the primary school in Hammersmith for ever, and had always taken it for granted that he would move away from it when the rest of his class moved at eleven. He felt, without actually being able to recall the relevant conversation, that his mother had quite definitely implied this. But it didn't work out like that. 'You should go in September,' his father said, that was that.

'Oh, darling,' his mother murmured when the arrangements had all been made. 'Oh, Michael, I'll miss you.'

His father would pay the fees and his father would in future give him pocket-money, over and above what his mother gave him. He'd like it at Elton Grange, his father promised. 'Oh yes, you'll like it,' his mother said too.

She was a woman of medium height, five foot four, with a round, plump face and plump arms and legs. There was a soft prettiness about her, about her light-blue eyes and her wide, simple mouth and her fair, rather fluffy hair. Her hands were always warm, as if expressing the warmth of her nature. She wept easily and often said she was silly to weep so. She talked a lot, getting carried away when she didn't watch herself: for this failing, too, she regularly said she was silly. 'Mrs Silly', she used to say when Michael was younger, condemning herself playfully for the two small follies she found it hard to control.

She worked as a secretary for an Indian, a Mr Ashaf, who had an office-stationery business. There was the shop – more of a warehouse, really – with stacks of swivel chairs and filing-cabinets on top of one another and green metal desks, and cartons containing continuation paper and top-copy foolscap and flimsy, and printed invoices. There were other cartons full of envelopes, and packets of paper-clips, drawing-pins and staples. The carbon-paper supplies were kept in the office behind the shop, where Michael's mother sat in front of a typewriter, typing invoices mainly. Mr Ashaf, a small wiry man, was always on his feet, moving between the shop and the office, keeping an eye on Michael's mother and on Dolores Welsh who looked after the retail side. Before she'd married, Michael's mother had been a secretary in the Wedgwood Centre, but returning to work at the time of her divorce she'd found it more convenient to work for Mr Ashaf since his premises were only five minutes away from where she and Michael lived. Mr Ashaf was happy to employ her on the kind of part-time basis that meant she could be at home every afternoon by the time Michael got in from school. During the holidays Mr Ashaf permitted her to take the typewriter to her flat, to come in every morning to collect what work there was and hand over what she'd done the day before. When this arrangement wasn't convenient, due to the nature of the work, Michael accompanied her to Mr Ashaf's premises and sat in the office with her or with Dolores Welsh in the shop. Mr Ashaf used occasionally to give him a sweet.

'Perhaps I'll change my job,' Michael's mother said brightly, a week before he was due to become a boarder at Elton Grange. 'I could maybe go back to the West End. Nice to have a few more pennies.' She was cheering herself up – he could tell by the way she looked at him. She packed his belongings carefully, giving him many instructions about looking after himself, about keeping himself warm and changing any clothes that got wet. 'Oh, darling,' she said at Paddington on the afternoon of his departure. 'Oh, darling, I'll miss you so!'

He would miss her, too. Although his father and Gillian were in every way more fun than his mother, it was his mother he loved. Although she fussed and was a nuisance sometimes, there was always the warmth, the cosiness of climbing into her bed on Sunday mornings or watching Magic Roundabout together. He was too big for Magic Roundabout now, or so he considered, and he rather thought he was too big to go on climbing into her bed. But the memories of all this cosiness had become part of his relationship with her.

She wept as they stood together on the platform. She held him close to her, pressing his head against her breast. 'Oh, darling!' she said. 'Oh, my darling.'

Her tears damped his face. She sniffed and sobbed, whispering that she didn't know what she'd do. 'Poor thing!' someone passing said. She blew her nose. She apologised to Michael, trying to smile. 'Remember where your envelopes are,' she said. She'd addressed and stamped a dozen envelopes for him so that he could write to her. She wanted him to write at once, just to say he'd arrived safely.

'And don't be homesick now,' she said, her own voice trembling again. 'Big boy, Michael.'

The train left her behind. He waved from the corridor window, and she gestured at him, indicating that he shouldn't lean out. But because of the distances between them he couldn't understand what the gesture meant. When the train stopped at Reading he found his writing-paper and envelopes in his overnight bag and began to write to her.

***

At Elton Grange he was in the lowest form, Miss Brooks's form. Miss Brooks, grey-haired at sixty, was the only woman on the teaching staff. She did not share the men's common-room but sat instead in the matrons' room, where she smoked Senior Service cigarettes between lessons. There was pale tobacco-tinged hair on her face, and on Tuesday and Friday afternoons she wore jodhpurs, being in charge of the school's riding. Brookie she was known as.

The other women at Elton Grange were Sister and the undermatron Miss Trenchard, the headmaster's wife Mrs Lyng, the lady cook Miss Arland, and the maids. Mrs Lyng was a stout woman, known among the boys as Outsize Dorothy, and Sister was thin and brisk. Miss Trenchard and Miss Arland were both under twenty-three; Miss Arland was pretty and Miss Trenchard wasn't. Miss Arland went about a lot with the history and geography master, Cocky Marshall, and Miss Trenchard was occasionally seen with the P.T. instructor, a Welshman, who was also in charge of the carpentry shop. Among the older boys Miss Trenchard was sometimes known as Tampax.

Twice a week Michael wrote to his mother, and on Sundays he wrote to his father as well. He told them that the headmaster was known to everyone as A.J.L. and he told them about the rules, how no boy in the three lower forms was permitted to be seen with his hands in his pockets and how no boy was permitted to run through A.J.L.'s garden. He said the food was awful because that was what everyone else said, although he quite liked it really.

At half-term his father and Gillian came. They stayed in the Grand, and Michael had lunch and tea there on the Saturday and on the Sunday, and just lunch on the Monday because they had to leave in the afternoon. He told them about his friends, Carson and Tichbourne, and his father suggested that next half-term Carson and Tichbourne might like to have lunch or tea at the Grand. 'Or maybe Swagger Browne,' Michael said. Browne's people lived in Kenya and his grandmother, with whom he spent the holidays, wasn't always able to come at half-term. 'Hard up,' Michael said.

Tichbourne and Carson were in Michael's dormitory, and there was one other boy, called Andrews: they were all aged eight. At night, after lights out, they talked about most things: about their families and the houses they lived in and the other schools they'd been at. Carson told about the time he'd put stink-bombs under the chair-legs when people were coming to play bridge, and Andrews about the time he'd been caught, by a policeman, stealing strawberries.

'What's it like?' Andrews asked in the dormitory one night. 'What's it like, a divorce?'

'D'you see your mother?' Tichbourne asked, and Michael explained that it was his mother he lived with, not his father.

'Often wondered what it's like for the kids,' Andrews said. 'There's a woman in our village who's divorced. She ran off with another bloke, only the next thing was he ran off with someone else.'

'Who'd your mum run off with?' Carson asked.

'No one.'

'Your dad run off then?'

'Yes.'

His mother had told him that his father left her because they didn't get on any more. He hadn't left her because he knew Gillian. He hadn't met Gillian for years after that.

'D'you like her?' Andrews asked. 'Gillian?'

'She's all right. They've got twins now, my dad and Gillian. Girls.'

'I'd hate it if my mum and dad got divorced,' Tichbourne said.

'Mine quarrelled all last holidays,' Carson said, 'about having a room decorated.'

'Can't stand it when they quarrel,' Andrews said.

Intrigued by a situation that was strange to them, the other boys often asked after that about the divorce. How badly did people have to quarrel before they decided on one? Was Gillian different from Michael's mother? Did Michael's mother hate her? Did she hate his father?

'They never see one another,' Michael said. 'She's not like Gillian at all.'

At the end of the term the staff put on a show called Staff Laughs. Cocky Marshall was incarcerated all during one sketch in a wooden container that was meant to be a steam bath. Something had gone wrong with it. The steam was too hot and the catch had become jammed. Cocky Marshall was red in the face and nobody knew if he was putting it on or not until the end of the sketch, when he stepped out of the container in his underclothes. Mr Waydelin had to wear a kilt in another sketch and Miss Arland and Miss Trenchard were dressed up in rugby togs, with Cocky Marshall's and Mr Brine's scrum caps. The Reverend Green – mathematics and divinity – was enthusiastically applauded in his Mrs Wagstaffe sketch. A.J.L. did his magic, and as a grand finale the whole staff, including Miss Brooks, sang together, arm-in-arm, on the small stage. 'We're going home,' they sang. 'We're going home. We're on the way that leads to home. We've seen the good things and the bad and now we're absolutely mad. We're g-o-i-n-g home.' All the boys joined in the chorus, and that night in Michael's dormitory they ate Crunchie, Galaxy and Mars Bars and didn't wash their teeth afterwards. At half past twelve the next day Michael's mother was waiting for him at Paddington. ▌

***

At home, nothing was different. On Saturdays his father came and drove him away to the house near Cranleigh. His mother talked about Dolores Welsh and Mr Ashaf. She hadn't returned to work in the West End. It was quite nice really, she said, at Mr Ashaf's.

Christmas came and went. His father gave him a new Triang locomotive and Gillian gave him a pogo-stick and the twins a magnet and a set of felt pens. His mother decorated the flat and put fairy-lights on a small Christmas tree. She filled his stocking on Christmas Eve when he was asleep and the next day, after they'd had their Christmas dinner, she gave him a football and a glove puppet and a jigsaw of Windsor Castle. He gave her a brooch he'd bought in Woolworth's. On January 14th he returned to Elton Grange.

***

Nothing was different at Elton Grange either, except that Cocky Marshall had left. Nobody had known he was going to leave, and some boys said he had been sacked. But others denied that, claiming that he'd gone of his own accord, without giving the required term's notice. They said A.J.L. was livid.

Three weeks passed, and then one morning Michael received a letter from his father saying that neither he nor Gillian would be able to come at half-term because he had to go to Tunisia on business and wanted to take Gillian with him. He sent some money to make up for the disappointment.

In a letter to his mother, not knowing what to say because nothing much was happening, Michael revealed that his father wouldn't be there at half-term. *Then I shall come*, his mother wrote back.

***

She stayed, not in the Grand, but in a boarding-house called Sans Souci, which had coloured gnomes fishing in a pond in the front garden, and a black gate with one hinge broken. They weren't able to have lunch there on the Saturday because the woman who ran it, Mrs Malone didn't do lunches. They had lunch in the Copper Kettle, and since Mrs Malone didn't do teas either they had tea in the Copper Kettle as well. They walked around the town between lunch and tea, and after tea they sat together in his mother's bedroom until it was time to catch the bus back to school.

The next day she said she'd like to see over the school, so he brought her into the chapel, which once had been the gate-lodge, and into the classrooms and the gymnasium and the art-room and the changing-rooms. In the carpentry shop the P.T. instructor was making a cupboard. 'Who's that boy?' his mother whispered, unfortunately just loud enough for the P.T.

instructor to hear. He smiled. Swagger Browne, who was standing about doing nothing, giggled.

'But how could he be a boy?' Michael asked, dismally leading the way on the cinder path that ran around the cricket pitch. 'Boys at Elton only go up to thirteen and a half.'

'Oh dear, of course,' his mother said. She began to talk of other things. She spoke quickly. Dolores Welsh, she thought, was going to get married, Mr Ashaf had wrenched his arm. She'd spoken to the landlord about the damp that kept coming in the bathroom, but the landlord had said that to cure it would mean a major upheaval for them.

All the time she was speaking, while they walked slowly on the cinder path, he kept thinking about the P.T. instructor, unable to understand how his mother could ever have mistaken him for a boy. It was a cold morning and rather damp, not raining heavily, not even drizzling, but misty in a particularly wetting kind of way. He wondered where they were going to go for lunch, since the woman in the Copper Kettle had said yesterday that the cafe didn't open on Sundays.

'Perhaps we could go and look at the dormitories?' his mother suggested when they came to the end of the cinder path.

He didn't want to, but for some reason he felt shy about saying so. If he said he didn't want to show her the dormitories, she'd ask him why and he wouldn't know what to say because he didn't know himself.

'All right,' he said.

They walked through the dank mist, back to the school buildings, which were mostly of red brick, some with a straggle of Virginia creeper on them. The new classrooms, presented a year ago by the father of a boy who had left, were of pinker brick than the rest. The old classrooms had been nicer, Michael's father said: they'd once been the stables.

There were several entrances to the house itself. The main one, approached from the cricket pitch by crossing A.J.L.'s lawns and then crossing a large, almost circular gravel expanse, was grandiose in the early Victorian style. Stone pillars supported a wide gothic arch through which, in a sizeable vestibule, further pillars framed a heavy oak front door. There were croquet mallets and hoops in a wooden box in this vestibule, and deck-chairs and two coloured golfing umbrellas. There was an elaborate wrought-iron scraper and a revolving brush for taking the mud from shoes and boots. On either side of the large hall door there was a round window, composed of circular, lead-encased panes. 'Well, at least they haven't got rid of those,' Michael's father had said, for these circular windows were a feature that boys who had been to Elton Grange often recalled with affection.

The other entrances to the house were at the back and it was through one of these, leading her in from the quadrangle and the squat new classrooms, past the kitchens and the staff lavatory, that Michael directed his mother on their way to the dormitories. All the other places they'd visited had been outside the house itself – the gymnasium and the changing-rooms were converted outbuildings, the carpentry shop was a wooden shed tucked neatly out of the way beside the garages, the art-room was an old conservatory, and the classroom block stood on its own, forming two sides of the quadrangle.

'What a nice smell!' Michael's mother whispered as they passed the kitchens, as Michael pressed himself against the wall to let Miss Brooks, in her jodhpurs, go by. Miss Brooks was carrying a riding stick and had a cigarette going. She didn't smile at Michael, nor at Michael's mother.

They went up the back stairs and Michael hoped they wouldn't meet anyone else. All the boys, except the ones like Swagger Browne whose people lived abroad, were out with their parents and usually the staff went away at half-term, if they possibly could. But A.J.L. and Outsize Dorothy never went away, nor did Sister, and Miss Trenchard had been there at prayers.

'How ever do you find your way through all these passages?' his mother whispered as he led her expertly towards his dormitory. He explained, in a low voice also, that you got used to the passages.

'Here it is,' he said, relieved to find that neither Sister nor Miss Trenchard was laying out clean towels. He closed the door behind them. 'That's my bed there,' he said.

He stood against the door with his ear cocked while she went to the bed and looked at it. She turned and smiled at him, her head a little on one side. She opened a locker and looked inside, but he explained that the locker she was looking in was Carson's. 'Where'd that nice rug come from?' she asked, and he said that he'd written to Gillian to say he'd been cold once or twice at night, and she'd sent him the rug immediately. 'Oh,' his mother said dispiritedly. 'Well, that was nice of Gillian,' she added.

She crossed to one of the windows and looked down over A.J.L.'s lawns to the chestnut trees that surrounded the playing-fields. It really was a beautiful place, she said.

She smiled at him again and he thought, what he'd never thought before, that her clothes were cheap-looking. Gillian's clothes were clothes you somehow didn't notice: it didn't occur to you to think they were cheap-looking or expensive. The women of Elton Grange all dressed differently, Outsize Dorothy in woollen things, Miss Brooks in suits, with a tie, and Sister and Miss Trenchard and Miss Arland always had white coats, the maids wore blue overalls most of the time but sometimes you saw them going home in the evenings in their ordinary clothes, which you never really thought about and certainly you never thought were cheap-looking.

'Really beautiful,' she said, still smiling, still at the window. She was wearing a headscarf and a maroon coat and another scarf at her neck. Her handbag was maroon also, but it was old, with something broken on one of the buckles: it was the handbag, he said to himself, that made you think she was cheaply dressed.

He left the door and went to her, taking her arm. He felt ashamed that he'd thought her clothes were cheap-looking. She'd been upset when he'd told her that the rug had been sent by Gillian. She'd been upset and he hadn't bothered.

'Oh, Mummy,' he said.

She hugged him to her, and when he looked up into her face he saw the mark of a tear on one of her cheeks. Her fluffy hair was sticking out a bit beneath the headscarf, her round, plump face was forcing itself to smile.

'I'm sorry,' he said.

'Sorry? Darling, there's no need.'

'I'm sorry you're left all alone there, Mummy.'

'Oh, but I'm not at all. I've got the office every day, and one of these days

I really will see about going back to the West End. We've been awfully busy at the office, actually, masses to do.'

The sympathy he'd showed caused her to talk. Up to now – ever since they'd met the day before – she'd quite deliberately held herself back in this respect, knowing that to chatter on wouldn't be the thing at all. Yesterday she'd waited until she'd returned to Sans Souci before relaxing. She'd had a nice long chat with Mrs Malone on the landing, which unfortunately had been spoiled by a man in one of Mrs Malone's upper rooms poking his head out and asking for a bit of peace. 'Sorry about that,' she'd heard Mrs Malone saying to him later. 'Couldn't really stop her' – a statement that had spoiled things even more. 'I'm ever so sorry,' she'd said quietly to Mrs Malone at breakfast.

'Let's go down now,' Michael said.

But his mother didn't hear this remark, engaged as she was upon making a series of remarks herself. She was no longer discreetly whispering, but chattering on with even more abandon than she had displayed on Mrs Malone's stairs the night before. A flush had spread over her cheeks and around her mouth and on the portion of her cheek which could be seen above her scarf. Michael could see she was happy.

'We'll have to go to Dolores' wedding,' she said. 'On the 8th. The 8th of May, a Thursday I think it is. They're coming round actually, Dolores and her young chap, Brian Haskins he's called. Mr Ashaf says he wouldn't trust him, but actually Dolores is no fool.'

'Let's go down now, Mum.'

She said she'd like to see the other dormitories. She'd like to see the senior dormitories, into one of which Michael would eventually be moving. She began to talk about Dolores Welsh and Brian Haskins again and then about Mrs Malone, and then about a woman Michael had never heard of before, a person called Peggy Urch.

He pointed out that the dormitories were called after imperial heroes. His was Drake, others were Raleigh, Nelson, Wellington, Marlborough and Clive. 'I think I'll be moving to Nelson,' Michael said. 'Or Marlborough. Depends.' But he knew she wasn't listening, he knew she hadn't taken in the fact that the dormitories were named like that. She was talking about Peggy Urch when he led her into Marlborough. Outsize Dorothy was there with

Miss Trenchard, taking stuff out of Verschoyle's locker because Verschoyle had just gone to the sanatorium.

'Very nice person,' Michael's mother was saying. 'She's taken on the Redmans' flat – the one above us, you know.'

It seemed to Michael that his mother didn't see Outsize Dorothy and Miss Trenchard. It seemed to him for a moment that his mother didn't quite know where she was.

'Looking for me?' Outsize Dorothy said. She smiled and waddled towards them. She looked at Michael, waiting for him to explain who this visitor was. Miss Trenchard looked, too.

'It's my mother,' he said, aware that these words were inept and inelegant.

'I'm Mrs Lyng,' Outsize Dorothy said. She held out her hand and Michael's mother took it.

'The Matron,' she said. 'I've heard of you, Mrs Lyng.'

''Well actually,' Outsize Dorothy contradicted with a laugh, 'I'm the headmaster's wife.' All the flesh on her body wobbled when she laughed. Tichbourne said he knew for a fact she was twenty stone.

'What a lovely place you have, Mrs Lyng. I was just saying to Michael. What a view from the windows!'

Outsize Dorothy told Miss Trenchard to go on getting Verschoyle's things together, in a voice that implied that Miss Trenchard wasn't paid to stand about doing nothing in the dormitories. All the women staff – the maids and Sister and Miss Arland and Miss Trenchard – hated Outsize Dorothy because she'd expect them, even Sister, to go on rooting in a locker while she talked to a parent. She wouldn't in a million years say: 'This is Miss Trenchard, the undermatron.'

'Oh, I'm afraid we don't have much time for views at Elton,' Outsize Dorothy said. She was looking puzzled, and Michael imagined she was thinking that his mother was surely another woman, a thinner, smarter, quieter person. But then Outsize Dorothy wasn't clever, as she often light-heartedly said herself, and was probably saying to herself that she must be confusing one boy's mother with another.

'Dorothy!' a voice called out, a voice which Michael instantly and to his horror recognized as A.J.L.'s.

'We had such a view at home!' Michael's mother said. 'Such a gorgeous view!' She was referring to her own home, a rectory in Somerset somewhere. She'd often told Michael about the rectory and the view, and her parents, both dead now. Her father had received the call to the Church late in life: he'd been in the Customs and Excise before that.

'Here, dear,' Outsize Dorothy called out. 'In Marlborough.'

Michael knew he'd gone red in the face. His stomach felt hot also, the palms of his hands were clammy. He could hear the clatter of the headmaster's footsteps on the uncarpeted back stairs. He began to pray, asking for something to happen, anything at all, anything God could think of.

His mother was more animated than before. More fluffy hair had slipped out from beneath her headscarf, the flush had spread over a greater area of her face. She was talking about the lack of view from the flat where she and Michael lived in Hammersmith, and about Peggy Urch who'd come to live in the flat directly above them and whose view was better because she could see over the poplars.

'Hullo,' A.J.L. said, a stringy, sandy man, the opposite of Outsize Dorothy and in many ways the perfect complement. Tichbourne said he often imagined them naked in bed, A.J.L. winding his stringiness around her explosive bulk.

Hands were shaken again. 'Having a look round?' A.J.L. said. 'Staying at the Grand?'

Michael's mother said she wasn't staying at the Grand but at Sans Souci, did he know it? They'd been talking about views, she said, it was lovely to have a room with a view, she hoped Michael wasn't giving trouble, her husband of course – well, ex-husband now – had been to this school in his time, before going on to Radley. Michael would probably go to Radley too.

'Well, we hope so,' A.J.L. said, seizing the back of Michael's neck. 'Shown her the new classrooms, eh?'

'Yes, sir.'

'Shown her where we're going to have our swimming-pool?'

'Not yet, sir.'

'Well, then.'

His mother spoke of various diseases Michael had had, measles and whooping cough and chicken-pox, and of diseases he hadn't had, mumps in particular. Miss Trenchard was like a ghost, all in white, still sorting out the junk in Verschoyle's locker, not daring to say a word. She was crouched there, with her head inside the locker, listening to everything.

'Well, we mustn't keep you,' A.J.L. said, shaking hands again with Michael's mother. 'Always feel free to come.'

There was such finality about these statements, more in the headmaster's tone than in the words themselves, that Michael's mother was immediately silent. The statements had a physical effect on her, as though quite violently they had struck her across the face. When she spoke again it was in the whisper she had earlier employed

'I'm sorry,' she said. 'I'm ever so sorry for going on so.'

A.J.L. and Outsize Dorothy laughed, pretending not to understand what she meant. Miss Trenchard would tell Miss Arland. Sister would hear and so would Brookie, and the P.T. instructor would say that this same woman had imagined him to be one of the boys. Mr Waydelin would hear, and Square-jaw Simpson – Cocky Marshall's successor – and Mr Brine and the Reverend Green.

'I have enjoyed it,' Michael's mother whispered. 'So nice to meet you.'

He went before her down the back stairs. His face was still red. They passed by the staff lavatory and the kitchens, out on to the concrete quadrangle. It was still misty and cold.

'I bought things for lunch,' she said, and for an awful moment he thought that she'd want to eat them somewhere in the school or in the grounds – in the art-room or the cricket pavilion. 'We could have a picnic in my room,' she said.

They walked down the short drive, past the chapel that once had been the gate-lodge. They caught a bus after a wait of half an hour, during which she began to talk again, telling him more about Peggy Urch, who reminded her of another friend she'd had once, a Margy Bassett. In her room in Sans

Souci she went on talking, spreading out on the bed triangles of cheese, and tomatoes and rolls and biscuits and oranges. They sat in her room when they'd finished, eating Rollo. At six o'clock they caught a bus back to Elton Grange. She wept a little when she said goodbye. ▐

***

Michael's mother did not, as it happened, ever arrive at Elton Grange at half-term again. There was no need for her to do so because his father and Gillian were always able to come themselves. For several terms he felt embarrassed in the presence of A.J.L. and outsize Dorothy and Miss Trenchard, but no one at school mentioned the unfortunate visit, not even Swagger Browne, who had so delightedly overheard her assuming the P.T. instructor to be one of the boys. School continued as before and so did the holidays, Saturdays in Cranleigh and the rest of the week in Hammersmith, news of Mr Ashaf and Dolores Welsh, now Dolores Haskins. Peggy Urch, the woman in the flat upstairs, often came down for a chat.

Often, too, Michael and his mother would sit together in the evenings on the sofa in front of the electric fire. She'd tell him about the rectory in Somerset and her father who had received the call to the Church late in his life, who'd been in the Customs and Excise. She'd tell him about her own childhood, and even about the early days of her marriage. Sometimes she wept a little, hardly at all, and he would take her arm on the sofa and she would smile and laugh. When they sat together on the sofa or went out together, to the cinema, or for a walk by the river or to the teashop called the Maids of Honour near Kew Gardens, Michael felt that he would never want to marry because he'd prefer to be with his mother. Even when she chatted on to some stranger in the Maids of Honour he felt he loved her: everything was different from the time she'd come to Elton Grange because away from Elton Grange things didn't matter in the same way.

Then something unpleasant threatened. During his last term at Elton Grange Michael was to be confirmed. 'Oh, but of course I must come,' his mother said.

It promised to be worse than the previous occasion. After the service you were meant to bring your parents in to tea in the Great Hall and see that they had a cup of tea and sandwiches and cakes. You had to introduce them to the Bishop of Bath and Wells. Michael imagined all that. In bed at night he imagined his father and Gillian looking very smart, his father chatting easily to Mr Brine, Gillian smiling at Outsize Dorothy, and his mother's hair fluffing out from beneath her headscarf. He imagined his mother and his father and Gillian having to sit together in a pew in chapel, as naturally they'd be expected to, being members of the same party.

'There's no need to,' he said in the flat in Hammersmith. 'There's really no need to, Mum.'

She didn't mention his father and Gillian, although he'd repeatedly said that they'd be there. It was as if she didn't want to think about them, as if she was deliberately pretending that they'd decided not to attend. She'd stay in Sans Souci again, she said. They'd have a picnic in her room, since the newly confirmed were to be excused school tea on the evening of the service. 'Dinner at the Grand, old chap,' his father said. 'Bring Tichbourne if you want to.'

Michael returned to Elton Grange at the end of the Easter holidays, leaving his mother in a state of high excitement at Paddington Station because she'd be seeing him again within five weeks. He thought he might invent an illness a day or two before the confirmation, or say at the last moment that he had doubts. In fact, he did hint to the Reverend Green that he wasn't certain about being quite ready for the occasion, but the Reverend Green sharply told him not to be silly. Every time he went down on his knees at the end of a session with the Reverend Green he prayed that God might come to his rescue. But God did not, and all during the night before the confirmation service he lay awake. It wasn't just because she was weepy and embarrassing, he thought: it was because she dressed in that cheap way, it was because she was common, with a common voice that wasn't at all like Gillian's or Mrs Tichbourne's or Mrs Carson's or even Outsize Dorothy's. He couldn't prevent these thoughts from occurring. Why couldn't she do something about her fluffy hair? Why did she have to gabble like that? 'I think I have a temperature,' he said in the morning, but when Sister took it it was only 98.

Before the service the other candidates waited outside the chapel to greet their parents and godparents, but Michael went into the chapel early and took up a devout position. Through his fingers he saw the Reverend Green lighting the candles and preparing the altar. Occasionally, the Reverend Green glanced at Michael, somewhat suspiciously.

'Defend, O Lord, this Thy child,' said the Bishop of Bath and Wells, and when Michael walked back to his seat he kept his head down, not wanting to see his parents and Gillian. They sang Hyrm 459. 'My God, accept,' sang Michael, 'my heart this day.'

He walked with Swagger Browne down the aisle, still with his eyes down. 'Fantastic,' said Swagger Browne outside the chapel, for want of anything better to say. 'Bloody fantastic.' They waited for the congregation to come out.

Michael had godparents, but his father had said that they wouldn't be able to attend. His godmother had sent him a prayer-book.

'Well done,' his father said. 'Well done, Mike.'

'What lovely singing!' Gillian murmured. She was wearing a white dress with a collar that was, slightly turned up, and a white wide-rimmed hat. On the gravel outside the chapel she put on dark glasses against the afternoon sun.

'Your mother's here somewhere,' his father said. 'You'd better see to her, Mike.' He spoke quietly, with a hand resting for a moment on Michael's shoulder. 'We'll be all right,' he added.

Michael turned. She was standing alone, as he knew she would be. Unable to prevent himself, he wished she wouldn't always wear head-scarves. 'Oh, darling,' she said.

She took his hands and pulled him towards her. She kissed him, apologising for the embrace but saying that it was a special occasion. She wished her father were alive, she said.

'Tea in the Great Hall,' A.J.L. was booming, and Outsize Dorothy was waddling about in flowered yellow, smiling at the faces of parents and godparents. 'Do come and have tea,' she gushed.

'Oh, I'd love a cup of tea,' Michael's mother whispered.

The crowd was moving through the sunshine, suited men, the Reverend Green in his cassock, the Bishop in crimson, women in their garden-party finery. They walked up the short drive from the chapel. They passed through the wide gothic arch that heralded the front door, through the vestibule where the croquet set was tidily in place and the deck-chairs neat against a wall. They entered what A.J.L. had years ago christened the Great

Hall, where buttered buns and sandwiches and cakes and sausage-rolls were laid out on trestle tables. Miss Trenchard and Miss Arland were in charge of two silver-plated tea-urns.

'I'll get you something to eat,' Michael said to his mother, leaving her although he knew she didn't want to be left. 'Seems no time since I was getting done myself,' he heard his father saying to A.J.L.

Miss Arland poured a cup of tea for his mother and told him to offer her something to eat. He chose a plate of sausage-rolls. She smiled at him. 'Don't go away again,' she whispered.

But he had to go away again because he couldn't stand there holding the sausage-rolls. He darted back to the table and left the plate there, taking one for himself. When he returned to his mother she'd been joined by the Reverend Green and the Bishop.

The Bishop shook Michael's hand and said it had been a very great pleasure to confirm him.

'My father was in the Church,' Michael's mother said, and Michael knew that she wasn't going to stop now. He watched her struggling to hold the words back, crumbling the pastry of her sausage-roll beneath her fingers. The flush had come into her cheeks, there was a brightness in her eyes. The Bishop's face was kind: she couldn't help herself, when kindness like that was there.

'We really must be moving,' the Reverend Green said, but the Bishop only smiled, and on and on she went about her father and the call he'd received so late in life. 'I'm sure you knew him, my lord,' was one suggestion she made, and the Bishop kindly agreed that he probably had.

'Mrs Grainer would like to meet the Bishop,' Outsize Dorothy murmured to the Reverend Green. She looked at Michael's mother and Michael could see her remembering her and not caring for her.

'Well, if you'll excuse us,' the Reverend Green said, seizing the Bishop's arm.

'Oh Michael dear, isn't that a coincidence!'

There was happiness all over her face, bursting from her eyes, in her smile and her flushed cheeks and her fluffy hair. She turned to Mr and

Mrs Tichbourne, who were talking to Mrs Carson, and said the Bishop had known her father, apparently quite well. She hadn't even been aware that it was to be this particular bishop today, it hadn't even occurred to her while she'd been at the confirmation service that such a coincidence could be possible. Her father had passed away fifteen years ago, he'd have been a contemporary of the Bishop's. 'He was in the Customs and Excise,' she said, 'before he received the call.'

They didn't turn away from her. They listened, putting in a word or two, about coincidences and the niceness of the Bishop. Tichbourne and Carson stood eating sandwiches, offering them to one another. Michael's face felt like a bonfire.

'We'll probably see you later,' Mr Tichbourne said, eventually edging his wife away. 'We're staying at the Grand.'

'Oh no, I'm at Sans Souci. Couldn't ever afford the Grand!' She laughed.

'Don't think we know the Sans Souci,' Mrs Tichbourne said.

'Darling, I'd love another cup of tea,' his mother said to Michael, and he went away to get her one, leaving her with Mrs Carson. When he returned she was referring to Peggy Urch.

It was then, while talking to Mrs Carson, that Michael's mother fell. Afterwards she said that she'd felt something slimy under one of her heels and had moved to rid herself of it. The next thing she knew she was lying on her back on the floor, soaked in tea.

Mrs Carson helped her to her feet. A.J.L. hovered solicitously. Outsize Dorothy picked up the cup and saucer.

'I'm quite all right,' Michael's mother kept repeating. 'There was something slippy on the floor, I'm quite all right.'

She was led to a chair by A.J.L. 'I think we'd best call on Sister,' he said. 'Just to be sure.'

But she insisted that she was all right, that there was no need to go bothering Sister. She was as white as a sheet.

Michael's father and Gillian came up to her and said they were sorry. Michael could see Tichbourne and Carson nudging one another, giggling. For a moment he thought of running away, hiding in the attics or something. Half a buttered bun had got stuck to the sleeve of his mother's maroon coat when she'd fallen. Her left leg was saturated with tea.

'We'll drive you into town,' his father said. 'Horrible thing to happen.'

'It's just my elbow,' his mother whispered. 'I came down on my elbow.'

Carson and Tichbourne would imitate it because Carson and Tichbourne imitated everything. They'd stand there, pretending to be holding a cup of tea, and suddenly they'd be lying flat on their backs. 'I think we'd best call on Sister,' Carson would say, imitating A.J.L

His father and Gillian said goodbye to Outsize Dorothy and to A.J.L. His mother, reduced to humble silence again, seemed only to want to get away. In the car she didn't say anything at all and when they reached Sans Souci she didn't seem to expect Michael to go in with her. She left the car, whispering her thanks, a little colour gathering in her face again.

That evening Michael had dinner with Gillian and his father in the Grand. Tichbourne was there also, and Carson, and several other boys, all with their parents. 'I can drive a few of them back,' his father said, 'save everyone getting a car out.' He crossed the dining-room floor and spoke to Mr Tichbourne and Mr Carson and the father of a boy called Mallabedeely. Michael ate minestrone soup and chicken with peas and roast potatoes. Gillian told him what the twins had been up to and said his father was going to have a swimming-pool put in. His father returned to the table and announced that he'd arranged to drive everyone back at nine o' clock.

Eating his chicken, he imagined his mother in Sans Souci, sitting on the edge of the bed, probably having a cry. He imagined her bringing back to London the stuff she'd bought for a picnic in her room. She'd never refer to any of that, she'd never upbraid him for going to the Grand for dinner when she'd wanted him to be with her. She'd consider it just that she should be punished.

As they got into the car, his father said he'd drive round by Sans Souci so that Michael could run in for a minute. 'We're meant to be back by a quarter past,' Michael said quickly. 'I've said goodbye to her,' he added, which wasn't quite true.

It would perhaps have been different if Tichbourne and Carson hadn't been in the car. He'd have gone in and paused with her for a minute because he felt pity for her. But the unattractive facade of Sans Souci, the broken gate of the small front garden and the fishermen gnomes would have caused further nudging and giggling in his father's white Alfa-Romeo.

'You're sure now?' his father said. 'I'll get you there by a quarter past.'

'No, it's all right.'

She wouldn't be expecting him. She wouldn't even have unpacked the picnic she'd brought. ❚

'Hey, was that your godmother?' Tichbourne asked in the dormitory. 'The one who copped it on the floor?'

He began to shake his head and then he paused and went on shaking it. An aunt, he said, some kind of aunt, he wasn't sure what the relationship was. He hadn't thought of saying that before, yet it seemed so simple, and so right and so natural, that a distant aunt should come to a confirmation service and not stay, like everyone else, in the Grand. 'God, it was funny,' Carson said, and Tichbourne did his imitation, and Michael laughed with his friends. He was grateful to them for assuming that such a person could not be his mother. A.J.L. and Outsize Dorothy and Miss Trenchard knew she was his mother, and so did the Reverend Green, but for the remainder of his time at Elton Grange none of these people would have cause to refer to the fact in public. And if by chance A.J.L. did happen to say in class tomorrow that he hoped his mother was all right after her fall, Michael would say afterwards that A.J.L. had got it all wrong.

In the dark, he whispered to her in his mind. He said he was sorry, he said he loved her better than anyone.

I USED TO LIVE HERE ONCE

JEAN RHYS

> **Jean Rhys** (1890 – 1979) was born on the Caribbean island of Dominica and moved to England when she was 16 years old. She is best known for her novel, *Wide Sargasso Sea*, which offers a different perspective on the 'madwoman in the attic' character from Charlotte Bronte's *Jane Eyre*.
>
> 'I Used To Live Here Once', first published in 1976, like much of her work, explores what it feels like to be an outsider.

She was standing by the river looking at the stepping stones and remembering each one. There was the round unsteady stone, the pointed one, the flat one in the middle – the safe stone where you could stand and look around. The next wasn't so safe for when the river was full the water flowed over it and even when it showed dry it was slippery. But after that it was easy and soon she was standing on the other side.

The road was much wider than it used to be but the work had been done carelessly. The felled trees had not been cleared away and the bushes looked trampled. Yet it was the same road and she walked along feeling extraordinarily happy.

It was a fine day, a blue day. The only thing was that the sky had a glassy look that she didn't remember. That was the only word she could think of. Glassy. She turned the corner, saw that what had been the old pavé had been taken up, and there too the road was much wider, but it had the same unfinished look.

She came to the worn stone steps that led up to the house and her heart began to beat. The screw pine was gone, so was the mock summer house called the ajoupa, but the clove tree was still there and at the top of the steps the rough lawn stretched away, just as she remembered it. She stopped and looked towards the house that had been added to and painted white. It was strange to see a car standing in front of it.

There were two children under the big mango tree, a boy and a little girl, and she waved to them and called 'Hello' but they didn't answer her or turn their heads. Very fair children, as Europeans born in the West Indies so often are: as if the white blood is asserting itself against all odds.

The grass was yellow in the hot sunlight as she walked towards them. When she was quite close she called again, shyly: 'Hello.' Then, 'I used to live here once,' she said.

Still they didn't answer. When she said for the third time 'Hello' she was quite near them. Her arms went out instinctively with the longing to touch them.

It was the boy who turned. His grey eyes looked straight into hers. His expression didn't change. He said, 'Hasn't it gone cold all of a sudden. D'you notice? Let's go in.' 'Yes let's,' said the girl.

Her arms fell to her sides as she watched them running across the grass to the house. That was the first time she knew.

THE HITCH-HIKER

ROALD DAHL

Roald Dahl (1916-1990) is perhaps best known for children's classics such as *Charlie and the Chocolate Factory* and *Matilda*. However, he also wrote for adults, mainly short stories, and was famous for stories with an unexpected twist in the ending. 'The Hitch-hiker' was first published in 1977.

I had a new car. It was an exciting toy, a big BMW 3.3 Li, which means 3.3 litre, long wheelbase, fuel injection. It had a top speed of 129 mph and terrific acceleration. The body was pale blue. The seats inside were darker blue and they were made of leather, genuine soft leather of the finest quality. The windows were electrically operated and so was the sun-roof. The radio aerial popped up when I switched on the radio, and disappeared when I switched it off. The powerful engine growled and grunted impatiently at slow speeds, but at sixty miles an hour the growling stopped and the motor began to purr with pleasure.

I was driving up to London by myself. It was a lovely June day. They were haymaking in the fields and there were buttercups along both sides of the road. I was whispering along at seventy miles an hour, leaning back comfortably in my seat, with no more than a couple of fingers resting lightly on the wheel to keep her steady. Ahead of me I saw a man thumbing a lift. I touched the footbrake and brought the car to a stop beside him. I always stopped for hitch-hikers. I knew just how it used to feel to be standing on the side of a country road watching the cars go by. I hated the drivers for pretending they didn't see me, especially the ones in big cars with three empty seats. The large expensive cars seldom stopped. It was always the smaller ones that offered you a lift, or the old rusty ones, or the ones that were already crammed full of children and the driver would say, 'I think we can squeeze in one more.'

The hitch-hiker poked his head through the open window and said, 'Going to London, guv'nor?'

'Yes,' I said, 'jump in.'

He got in and I drove on.

He was a small ratty-faced man with grey teeth. His eyes were dark and quick and clever, like a rat's eyes, and his ears were slightly pointed at the top. He had a cloth cap on his head and he was wearing a greyish coloured jacket with enormous pockets. The grey jacket, together with the quick eyes and the pointed ears, made him look more than anything like some sort of a huge human rat. ||

'What part of London are you headed for?' I asked him.

'I'm goin' right through London and out the other side,' he said. 'I'm goin' to Epsom, for the races. It's Derby Day today.'

'So it is,' I said. 'I wish I were going with you. I love betting on horses.'

'I never bet on horses,' he said. 'I don't even watch 'em run. That's a stupid silly business.'

'Then why do you go?' I asked.

He didn't seem to like that question. His little ratty face went absolutely blank and he sat there staring straight ahead at the road, saying nothing.

'I expect you help to work the betting machines or something like that,' I said.

'That's even sillier,' he answered. 'There's no fun working them lousy machines and selling tickets to mugs. Any fool could do that.'

There was a long silence. I decided not to question him any more. I remembered how irritated I used to get in my hitch-hiking days when drivers kept asking me questions. Where are you going? Why are you going there? What's your job? Are you married? Do you have a girlfriend? What's her name? How old are you? And so on and so forth. I used to hate it.

'I'm sorry,' I said. 'It's none of my business what you do. The trouble is, I'm a writer, and most writers are terrible nosey parkers.'

'You write books?' he asked.

'Yes.'

'Writin' books is OK,' he said. 'It's what I call a skilled trade. I'm in a skilled trade too. The folks I despise is them that spend all their lives doin' crummy old routine jobs with no skill in 'em at all. You see what I mean?'

'Yes.'

'The secret of life,' he said, 'is to become very very good at somethin' that's very very 'ard to do.'

'Like you,' I said.

'Exactly. You and me both.'

'What makes you think that I'm any good at my job?' I asked. 'There's an awful lot lot of bad writers around.'

'You wouldn't be drivin' about in a car like this if you weren't no good at it,' he answered. 'It must've cost a tidy packet, this little job.'

'It wasn't cheap.'

'What can she do flat out?' he asked.

'One hundred and twenty-nine miles an hour,' I told him.

'I'll bet she won't do it.'

'I bet she will.'

'All car makers is liars,' he said. 'You can buy any car you like and it'll never do what the makers say it will in the ads.'

'This one will.'

'Open 'er up then and prove it,' he said. 'Go on, guv'nor, open 'er right up and let's see what she'll do.'

There is a roundabout at Chalfont St Peter and immediately beyond it there's a long straight section of dual carriageway. We came out of the roundabout on to the carriageway and I pressed my foot down on the accelerator. The big car leaped forwards as though she'd been stung. In ten seconds or so, we were doing ninety.

'Lovely!' he cried. 'Beautiful! Keep goin'!'

I had the accelerator jammed right down against the floor and I held it there.

'One hundred!' he shouted... 'A hundred and five!... A hundred and ten!... A hundred and ten!... A hundred and fifteen! Go on! Don't slack off!'

I was in the outside lane and we flashed past several cars as though they were standing still – a green Mini, a big cream-coloured Citroen, a white Land Rover, a huge truck with a container on the back, an orange-coloured Volkswagen Minibus...

'A hundred and twenty!' my passenger shouted, jumping up and down. 'Go on! Go on! Get'er'up to one-two-nine!'

At that moment, I heard the scream of a police siren. It was so loud it seemed to be right inside the car, and then a policeman on a motor-cycle loomed up alongside us on the inside lane and went past us and raised a hand for us to stop.

'Oh, my sainted aunt!' I said. 'That's torn it!'

The policeman must have been doing about a hundred and thirty when he passed us, and he took plenty of time slowing down. Finally, he pulled into the side of the road and I pulled in behind him. 'I didn't know police motor-cycles could go as fast as that,' I said rather lamely.

'That one can,' my passenger said. 'It's the same make as yours. It's a BMW R90S. Fastest bike on the road. That's what they're usin' nowadays.'

The policeman got off his motor-cycle and leaned the machine sideways on to its prop stand. Then he took off his gloves and placed them carefully on the seat. He was in no hurry now. He had us where he wanted us and he knew it.

'This is real trouble,' I said. 'I don't like it one bit.'

'Don't talk to 'im any more than is necessary, you understand,' my companion said. 'Just sit tight and keep mum.'

Like an executioner approaching his victim, the policeman came strolling slowly towards us. He was a big meaty man with a belly, and his blue breeches were skintight around his enormous thighs. His goggles were pulled up on the helmet, showing a smouldering red face with wide cheeks.

We sat there like guilty schoolboys, waiting for him to arrive.

'Watch out for this man,' my passenger whispered. ''Ee looks mean as the devil.'

The policeman came round to my open window and placed one meaty hand on the sill. 'What's the hurry?' he said.

'No hurry, officer,' I answered.

'Perhaps there's a woman in the back having a baby and you're rushing her to hospital? Is that it?'

'No, officer.'

'Or perhaps your house is on fire and you're dashing home to rescue the family from upstairs?' His voice was dangerously soft and mocking.

'My house isn't on fire, officer.'

'In that case,' he said, 'you've got yourself into a nasty mess, haven't you? Do you know what the speed limit is in this country?'

'Seventy,' I said.

'And do you mind telling me exactly what speed you were doing just now?'

I shrugged and didn't say anything.

When he spoke next, he raised his voice so loud that I jumped. '*One hundred and twenty miles per hour!*' he barked. 'That's *fifty* miles an hour over the limit!'

He turned his head and spat out a big gob of spit. It landed on the wing of my car and started sliding down over my beautiful blue paint. Then he turned back again and stared hard at my passenger. 'And who are you?' he asked sharply.

'He's a hitch-hiker,' I said. 'I'm giving him a lift.'

'I didn't ask you,' he said. 'I asked him.'

''Ave I done somethin' wrong?' my passenger asked. His voice was as soft and oily as haircream.

'That's more than likely,' the policeman answered. 'Anyway, you're a witness. I'll deal with you in a minute. Driving-licence,' he snapped, holding out his hand.

I gave him my driving-licence.

He unbuttoned the left-hand breast-pocket of his tunic and brought out the dreaded book of tickets. Carefully, he copied the name and address from my licence. Then he gave it back to me. He strolled round to the front of the car and read the number from the number-plate and wrote that down as well. He filled in the date, the time and the details of my offence. Then he tore out the top copy of the ticket. But before handing it to me, he checked that all the information had come through clearly on his own carbon copy. Finally, he replaced the book in his tunic pocket and fastened the button.

'Now you,' he said to my passenger, and he walked around to the other side of the car. From the other breast-pocket he produced a small black notebook. 'Name?' he snapped.

'Michael Fish,' my passenger said.

'Address?'

'Fourteen, Windsor Lane, Luton.'

'Show me something to prove this is your real name and address,' the policeman said.

My passenger fished in his pockets and came out with a driving-licence of his own. The policeman checked the name and address and handed it back to him. 'What's your job?' he asked sharply.

'I'm an 'od carrier.'

'A what?'

'An 'od carrier.'

'Spell it.'

'H-O-D C-A-...'

'That'll do. And what's a hod carrier may I ask?'

'An 'od carrier, officer, is a person 'oo carries the cement up the ladder to the bricklayer. And the 'od is what 'ee carries it in. It's got a long 'andle, and on the top you've got two bits of wood set at an angle...'

'All right, all right. Who's your employer?'

'Don't 'ave one. I'm unemployed.'

The policeman wrote all this down in the black note-book. Then he returned the book to its pocket and did up the button.

'When I get back to the station I'm going to do a little checking up on you,' he said to my passenger.

'Me? What've I done wrong?' the rat-faced man asked.

'I don't like your face, that's all,' the policeman said. 'And we just might have a picture of it somewhere in our files.' He strolled round the car and returned to my window.

'I suppose you know you're in serious trouble,' he said to me.

'Yes, officer.'

'You won't be driving this fancy car of yours again for a very long time, not after *we've* finished with you. You won't be driving *any* car again come to that for several years. And a good thing, too. I hope they lock you up for a spell into the bargain.'

'You mean prison?' I asked, alarmed.

'Absolutely,' he said, smacking his lips. 'In the clink. Behind the bars. Along with all the other criminals who break the law. *And* a hefty fine into the bargain. Nobody will be more pleased about that than me. I'll see you in court, both of you. You'll be getting a summons to appear.'

He turned away and walked over to his motor-cycle. He flipped the prop stand back into position with his foot and swung his leg over the saddle. Then he kicked the starter and roared off up the road out of sight. ▮

'Phew!' I gasped. 'That's done it.'

'We was caught,' my passenger said. 'We was caught good and proper.'

'I was caught, you mean.'

'That's right,' he said. 'What you goin' to do now, guv'nor?'

'I'm going straight up to London to talk to my solicitor,' I said. I started the car and drove on.

'You mustn't believe what 'ee said to you about goin' to prison,' my passenger said. 'They don't put nobody in the clink just for speedin'.'

'Are you sure of that?' I asked.

'I'm positive,' he answered. 'They can take your licence away and they can give you a whoppin' big fine, but that'll be the end of it.'

I felt tremendously relieved.

'By the way,' I said, 'why did you lie to him?'

'Who, me?' he said. 'What makes you think I lied?'

'You told him you were an unemployed hod carrier. But you told *me* you were in a highly skilled trade.'

'So I am,' he said. 'But it don't pay to tell everythin' to a copper.'

'So what *do* you do?' I asked him.

'Ah,' he said slyly. 'That'd be tellin', wouldn't it?'

'Is it something you're ashamed of?'

'Ashamed?' he cried. 'Me, ashamed of my job? I'm about as proud of it as anybody could be in the entire world!'

'Then why won't you tell me?'

'You writers really is nosey parkers, aren't you?' he said. 'And you ain't goin' to be 'appy, I don't think, until you've found out exactly what the answer is?'

'I don't really care one way or the other,' I told him, lying.

He gave me a crafty little ratty look out of the sides of his eyes. 'I think you do care,' he said. 'I can see it in your face that you think I'm in some kind of a very peculiar trade and you're just achin' to know what it is.'

I didn't like the way he read my thoughts. I kept quiet and stared at the road ahead.

'You'd be right, too,' he went on. 'I *am* in a very peculiar trade. I'm in the queerest peculiar trade of 'em all.'

I waited for him to go on.

'That's why I 'as to be extra careful 'oo I'm talkin' to, you see. 'Ow am I to know, for instance, you're not another copper in plain clothes?'

'Do I look like a copper?'

'No,' he said. 'You don't. And you ain't. Any fool could tell that.'

He took from his pocket a tin of tobacco and a packet of cigarette papers and started to roll a cigarette. I was watching him out of the corner of one eye, and the speed with which he performed this rather difficult operation was incredible. The cigarette was rolled and ready in about five seconds. He ran his tongue along the edge of the paper, stuck it down and popped the cigarette between his lips. Then, as if from nowhere, a lighter appeared in his hand. The lighter flamed. The cigarette was lit. The lighter disappeared. It was altogether a remarkable performance.

'I've never seen anyone roll a cigarette as fast as that,' I said.

'Ah,' he said, taking a deep suck of smoke. 'So you noticed.'

'Of course I noticed. It was quite fantastic.'

He sat back and smiled. It pleased him very much that I had noticed how quickly he could roll a cigarette. You want to know what makes me able to do it?' he asked.

'Go on then.'

'It's because I've got fantastic fingers. These fingers of mine,' he said, holding up both hands high in front of him, 'are quicker and cleverer than the fingers of the best piano player in the world!'

'Are you a piano player?'

'Don't be daft,' he said. 'Do I look like a piano player?'

I glanced at his fingers. They were so beautifully shaped, so slim and long and elegant, they didn't seem to belong to the rest of him at all. They looked more like the fingers of a brain surgeon or a watchmaker.

'My job,' he went on, 'is a hundred times more difficult than playin' the piano. Any twerp can learn to do that. There's titchy little kids learnin' to play the piano in almost any 'ouse you go into these days. That's right, ain't it?'

'More or less,' I said.

'Of course it's right. But there's not one person in ten million can learn to do what I do. Not one in ten million! 'Ow about that?'

'Amazing,' I said.

'You're darn right it's amazin',' he said.

'I think I know what you do,' I said. 'You do conjuring tricks. You're a conjurer.'

'Me?' he snorted. 'A conjurer? Can you picture me goin' round crummy kids' parties makin' rabbits come out of top 'ats?'

'Then you're a card player. You get people into card games and deal yourself marvellous hands.'

'Me! A rotten card-sharper!' he cried. 'That's a miserable racket if ever there was one.'

'All right. I give up.' ||

I was taking the car along slowly now, at no more than forty miles an hour, to make quite sure I wasn't stopped again. We had come on to the main London-Oxford road and were running down the hill towards Denham.

Suddenly, my passenger was holding up a black leather belt in his hand. 'Ever seen this before?' he asked. The belt had a brass buckle of unusual design.

'Hey!' I said. 'That's mine, isn't it? It *is* mine! Where did you get it?'

He grinned and waved the belt gently from side to side.

'Where d'you think I got it?' he said. 'Off the top of your trousers, of course.'

I reached down and felt for my belt. It was gone.

'You mean you took it off me while we've been driving along?' I asked, flabbergasted.

He nodded, watching me all the time with those little black ratty eyes.

'That's impossible,' I said. 'You'd have to undo the buckle and slide the whole thing out through the loops all the way round. I'd have seen you doing it. And even if I hadn't seen you, I'd have felt it.'

'Ah, but you didn't, did you?' he said triumphant. He dropped the belt on his lap and now all at once there was a brown shoelace dangling from his fingers. 'And what about this, then?' he exclaimed, waving the shoelace.

'What about it?' I said.

'Anyone round 'ere missin' a shoelace?' he asked, grinning.

I glanced down at my shoes. The lace of one of them was missing. 'Good grief!' I said. 'How did you do that? I never saw you bending down.'

'You never saw nothin',' he said proudly. 'You never even saw me move an inch. And you know why?'

'Yes,' I said. 'Because you've got fantastic fingers.'

'Exactly right!' he cried. 'You catch on pretty quick, don't you?' He sat back and sucked away at his home-made cigarette, blowing the smoke out in a thin stream against the windshield. He knew he had impressed me greatly with those two tricks, and this made him very happy. 'I don't want to be late,' he said. 'What time is it?'

'There's a clock in front of you,' I told him.

'I don't trust car clocks,' he said. 'What does your watch say?'

I hitched up my sleeve to look at the watch on my wrist. It wasn't there. I looked at the man. He looked back at me, grinning.

'You've taken that, too,' I said.

He held out his hand and there was my watch lying in his palm. 'Nice bit of stuff, this,' he said. 'Superior, quality. Eighteen-carat gold. Easy to flog, too. It's never any trouble gettin' rid of quality goods.'

'I'd like it back, if you don't mind,' I said rather huffily.

He placed the watch carefully on the leather tray in front of him. 'I wouldn't nick anything from you, guv'nor,' he said. 'You're my pal. You're giving me a lift.'

'I'm glad to hear it,' I said.

'All I'm doin' is answerin' your questions,' he went on. 'You asked me what I did for a livin' and I'm showin' you.'

'What else have you got of mine?'

He smiled again, and now he started to take from the pocket of his jacket one thing after another that belonged to me – my driving-licence, a key-ring with four keys on it, some pound notes, a few coins, a letter from my publishers, my diary, a stubby old pencil, a cigarette-lighter, and last of all, a beautiful old sapphire ring with pearls around it belonging to my wife. I was taking the ring up to the jeweller in London because one of the pearls was missing.

'Now *there's* another lovely piece of goods,' he said, turning the ring over in his fingers. 'That's eighteenth century, if I'm not mistaken, from the reign of King George the Third.'

You're right,' I said, impressed. 'You're absolutely right.'

He put the ring on the leather tray with the other items.

'So you're a pickpocket,' I said.

'I don't like that word,' he answered. 'It's a coarse and vulgar word. Pickpockets is coarse and vulgar people who only do easy little amateur jobs. They lift money from blind old ladies.'

'What do you call yourself, then?'

'Me? I'm a fingersmith. I'm a professional fingersmith.' He spoke the words solemnly and proudly, as though he were telling me he was the President of the Royal College of Surgeons or the Archbishop of Canterbury.

'I've never heard that word before,' I said. 'Did you invent it?'

'Of course I didn't invent it,' he replied. 'It's the name given to them who's risen to the very top of the profession. You've heard of a goldsmith and a silversmith, for instance. They're experts with gold and silver. I'm an expert with my fingers, so I'm a fingersmith.'

'It must be an interesting job.'

'It's a marvellous job,' he answered. 'It's lovely.'

'And that's why you go to the races?'

'Race meetings is easy meat,' he said. 'You just stand around after the race watchin' for the lucky ones to queue up and draw their money. And when you see someone collectin' a big bundle of notes, you simply follows after 'em and 'elps yourself. But don't get me wrong, guv'nor. I never takes nothin' from a loser. Nor from poor people neither. I only go after them as can afford it, the winners and the rich.'

'That's very thoughtful of you,' I said. 'How often do you get caught?'

'Caught?' he cried, disgusted. '*Me* get caught! It's only pickpockets get caught. Fingersmiths never. Listen, I could take the false teeth out of your mouth if I wanted to and you wouldn't even catch me!'

'I don't have false teeth,' I said.

'I know you don't,' he answered. 'Otherwise I'd 'ave 'ad 'em out long ago!'

I believed him. Those long slim fingers of his seemed able to do anything.

We drove on for a while without talking.

'That policeman's going to check up on you pretty thoroughly,' I said. 'Doesn't that worry you a bit?'

'Nobody's checkin' up on me,' he said.

'Of course they are. He's got your name and address written down most carefully in his black book.'

The man gave me another of his sly, ratty little smiles. 'Ah,' he said. 'So 'ee 'as. But I'll bet 'ee ain't got it all written down in 'is memory as well. I've never known a copper yet with a decent memory. Some of 'em can't even remember their own names.'

'What's memory got to do with it?' I asked. 'It's written down in his book, isn't it?'

'Yes, guv'nor, it is. But the trouble is, 'ee's lost the book. 'Ee's lost both books, the one with my name in it *and* the one with yours.'

In the long delicate fingers of his right hand, the man was holding up in triumph the two books he had taken from the policeman's pockets. 'Easiest job I ever done,' he announced proudly.

I nearly swerved the car into a milk-truck, I was so excited.

'That copper's got nothin' on either of us now,' he said.

'You're a genius!' I cried.

''Ee's got no names, no addresses, no car number, no nothin',' he said.

'You're brilliant!'

'I think you'd better pull in off this main road as soon as possible,' he said. 'Then we'd better build a little bonfire and burn these books.'

'You're a fantastic fellow,' I exclaimed.

'Thank you, guv'nor,' he said. 'It's always nice to be appreciated.'

TWO WORDS

ISABEL ALLENDE

Isabel Allende (1942-) is the multiple award-winning Chilean author of over 20 books, translated into 35 languages. She is an important figure among a group of South American writers of *magic realism*. This is a literary genre in which magic elements occur, as if naturally, in an otherwise normal environment.

'Two Words', first published in 1989, is a good example of magic realism and of Allende's rich use of language.

She went by the name of Belisa Crepusculario, not because she had been baptised with that name or given it by her mother, but because she herself had searched until she found the poetry of 'beauty' and 'twilight' and cloaked herself in it. She made her living selling words. She journeyed through the country from the high cold mountains to the burning coasts, stopping at fairs and in markets where she set up four poles covered by a canvas awning under which she took refuge from the sun and rain to minister to her customers. She did not have to peddle her merchandise because from having wandered far and near, everyone knew who she was. Some people waited for her from one year to the next, and when she appeared in the village with her bundle beneath her arm, they would form a line in front of her stall. Her prices were fair. For five centavos she delivered verses from memory; for seven she improved the quality of dreams; for nine she wrote love letters; for twelve she invented insults for irreconcilable enemies. She also sold stories, not fantasies but long, true stories she recited at one telling, never skipping a word. This is how she carried the news from one town to another. People paid her to add a line or two: our son was born; so and so died; our children got married; the crops burned in the field. Wherever she went a small crowd gathered around to listen as she began to speak, and that was how they learned about each others' doings, about distant relatives, about what was going on in the civil war. To anyone who paid her fifty centavos in trade, she gave the gift of a secret word to drive away melancholy. It was not the same word for everyone, naturally, because that would have been collective deceit. Each person received his or her own word, with the assurance that no one else would use it that way in this universe or the beyond. ▌

Belisa Crepusculario had been born into a family so poor they did not even have names to give their children. She came into the world and grew up in an inhospitable land where some years the rains became avalanches of water that bore everything away before them and others when not a drop fell from the sky and the sun swelled to fill the horizon and the world became a desert. Until she was twelve, Belisa had no occupation or virtue other than having withstood hunger and the exhaustion of centuries. During one interminable drought, it fell to her to bury four younger brothers and sisters; when she realised that her turn was next, she decided to set out across the plain in the direction of the sea, in hopes that she might trick death along the way. The land was eroded, split with deep cracks, strewn with rocks, fossils of trees and thorny bushes, and skeletons of animals bleached by the sun. From time to time she ran into families who, like her, were heading south, following the mirage of water. Some had begun the march carrying their belongings on their back or in small carts, but they could barely move their own bones, and after a while they had to abandon their possessions. They dragged themselves along painfully, their skin turned to lizard hide and their eyes burned by the reverberating glare. Belisa greeted them with a wave as she passed, but she did not stop, because she had no strength to waste in acts of compassion. Many people fell by the wayside, but she was so stubborn that she survived to cross through that hell and at long last reach the first trickles of water, fine, almost invisible threads that fed spindly vegetation and farther down widened into small streams and marshes.

Belisa Crepusculario saved her life and in the process accidentally discovered writing. In a village near the coast, the wind blew a page of newspaper at her feet. She picked up the brittle yellow paper and stood a long while looking at it, unable to determine its purpose, until curiosity overcame her shyness. She walked over to a man who was washing his horse in the muddy pool where she had quenched her thirst.

'What is this?' she asked.

'The sports page of the newspaper,' the man replied, concealing his surprise at her ignorance.

The answer astounded the girl, but she did not want to seem rude so she merely inquired about the significance of the fly tracks scattered across the page.

'Those are words, child. Here it says that Fulgenio Barba knocked out El Negro Tiznao in the third round.'

That was the day Belisa Crepusculario found out that words make their way in the world without a master, and that anyone with a little cleverness can appropriate them and do business with them. She made a quick assessment of her situation and concluded that aside from becoming a prostitute or working as a servant in the kitchens of the rich there were few occupations she was qualified for. It seemed to her that selling words would be an honourable alternative. From that moment on, she worked at that profession, and was never tempted by any other. At the beginning she offered her merchandise unaware that words could be written outside of newspapers. When she learned otherwise, she calculated the infinite possibilities of her trade and with her savings paid a priest twenty pesos to teach her to read and write; with her three remaining coins she bought a dictionary. She pored over it from A to Z and then threw it into the sea, because it was not her intention to defraud her customers with packaged words.

One August morning several years later, Belisa Crepusculario was sitting in her tent in the middle of a plaza, surrounded by the uproar of market day, selling legal arguments to an old man who had been trying for sixteen years to get his pension. Suddenly she heard yelling and thudding hoofbeats. She looked up from her writing and saw, first, a cloud of dust, and then a band of horsemen come galloping into the plaza. They were the Colonel's men, sent under orders of El Mulato, a giant known throughout the land for the speed of his knife and his loyalty to his chief. Both the Colonel and El Mulato had spent their lives fighting in the civil war, and their names were ineradicably linked to devastation and calamity. The rebels swept into town like a stampeding herd, wrapped in noise, bathed in sweat and leaving a hurricane of fear in their trail. Chickens took wing, dogs ran for their lives, women and children scurried out of sight, until the only living soul left in the market was Belisa Crepusculario. She had never seen El Mulato and was surprised to see him walking towards her.

'I'm looking for you,' he shouted, pointing his coiled whip at her; even before the words were out two men rushed her – knocking over her canopy and shattering her inkwell – bound her hand and foot, and threw her like a duffel bag across the rump of El Mulato's mount. Then they thundered off towards the hills.

Hours later, just as Belisa Crepusculario was near death, her heart ground to sand by the pounding of the horse, they stopped, and four strong hands set her down. She tried to stand on her feet and hold her head high, but her strength failed her and she slumped to the ground, sinking into a confused dream. She awakened several hours later to the murmur of night in the camp, but before she had time to sort out the sounds, she opened her eyes and found herself staring into the impatient glare of El Mulato, kneeling beside her.

'Well, woman, at last you have come to,' he said. To speed her to her senses, he tipped his canteen and offered her a sip of liquor laced with gunpowder.

She demanded to know the reason for such rough treatment, and El Mulato explained that the Colonel needed her services. He allowed her to splash water on her face, and then led her to the far end of the camp where the most feared man in all the land was lazing in a hammock strung between two trees. She could not see his face, because he lay in the deceptive shadow of the leaves and the indelible shadow of all his years as a bandit, but she imagined from the way his gigantic aide addressed him with such humility that he must have a very menacing expression. She was surprised by the Colonel's voice, as soft and well modulated as a professor's.

'Are you the woman who sells words?' he asked.

'At your service,' she stammered, peering into the dark and trying to see him better.

The Colonel stood up, and turned straight towards her. She saw dark skin and the eyes of a ferocious puma, and she knew immediately that she was standing before the loneliest man in the world.

'I want to be President,' he announced.

The Colonel was weary of riding across that godforsaken land, waging useless wars and suffering defeats that no subterfuge could transform into victories. For years he had been sleeping in the open air, bitten by mosquitoes, eating iguanas and snake soup, but these minor inconveniences were not why he wanted to change his destiny. What truly troubled him was the terror he saw in people's eyes. He longed to ride into a town beneath a triumphal arch with bright flags and flowers everywhere; he wanted to be cheered, and be given newly laid eggs and freshly baked bread. Men fled at the sight of him, children trembled, and women miscarried from fright; he had had enough, and so he had decided to become President. El Mulato had suggested that they ride to the capital, gallop up to the Palace, and take over the government, the way they had taken so many other things without anyone's permission. The Colonel, however, did not want to be just another tyrant; there had been enough of those before him and, besides, if he did that, he would never win people's hearts. It was his aspiration to win the popular vote in the December elections.

'To do that, I have to talk like a candidate. Can you sell me the words for a speech?' the Colonel asked Belisa Crepusculario.

She had accepted many assignments, but none like this. She did not dare refuse, fearing that El Mulato would shoot her between the eyes, or worse still, that the Colonel would burst into tears. There was more to it than that, however; she felt the urge to help him because she felt a throbbing warmth beneath her skin, a powerful desire to touch that man, to fondle him, to clasp him in her arms.

All night and a good part of the following day, Belisa Crepusculario searched her repertory for words adequate for a presidential speech, closely watched by El Mulato, who could not take his eyes from her firm wanderer's legs and virginal breasts. She discarded harsh, cold words, words that were too flowery, words worn from abuse, words that offered improbable promises, untruthful and confusing words, until all she had left were words sure to touch the minds of men and women's intuition. Calling upon the knowledge she had purchased from the priest for twenty pesos, she wrote the speech on a sheet of paper and then signalled El Mulato to untie the rope that bound her ankles to a tree. He led her once more to the Colonel, and again she felt the throbbing anxiety that had seized her when she first saw him. She handed him the paper and waited while he looked at it, holding it gingerly between thumbs and fingertips.

'What the shit does this say?' he asked finally.

'Don't you know how to read?'

'War's what I know,' he replied.

She read the speech aloud. She read it three times, so her client could engrave it on his memory. When she finished, she saw the emotion in the faces of the soldiers who had gathered round to listen, and saw that the Colonel's eyes glittered with enthusiasm, convinced that with those words the presidential chair would be his.

'If after they've heard it three times, the boys are still standing there with their mouths hanging open, it must mean the thing's damn good, Colonel,' was El Mulato's approval.

'All right, woman. How much do I owe you?' the leader asked.

'One peso, Colonel.'

'That's not much,' he said, opening the purse he wore at his belt, heavy with proceeds from the last foray.

'The peso entitles you to a bonus. I'm going to give you two secret words,' said Belisa Crepusculario.

'What for?'

She explained that for every fifty centavos a client paid, she gave him the gift of a word for his exclusive use. The Colonel shrugged. He had no interest at all in her offer, but he did not want to be impolite to someone who had served him so well. She walked slowly to the leather stool where he was sitting, and bent down to give him her gift. The man smelled the scent of a mountain cat issuing from the woman, a fiery heat radiating from her hips, he heard the terrible whisper of her hair, and a breath of sweet mint murmured into his ear the two secret words that were his alone.

'They are yours, Colonel,' she said as she stepped back. 'You may use them as much as you please.'

El Mulato accompanied Belisa to the roadside, his eyes as entreating as a stray dog's, but when he reached out to touch her, he was stopped by an avalanche of words he had never heard before; believing them to be an irrevocable curse, the flame of his desire was extinguished.

During the months of September, October and November, the Colonel delivered his speech so many times that had it not been crafted from glowing and durable words, it would have turned to ash as he spoke. He travelled up and down and across the country, riding into cities with a triumphal air, stopping in even the most forgotten villages where only the dump heap betrayed a human presence, to convince his fellow citizens to vote for him. While he spoke from a platform erected in the middle of the plaza, El Mulato and his men handed out sweets and painted his name on all the walls in gold frost. No one paid the least attention to those advertising ploys; they were dazzled by the clarity of the Colonel's proposals and the poetic lucidity of his arguments, infected by his powerful wish to right the wrongs of history, happy for the first time in their lives. When the Candidate had finished his speech, his soldiers would fire their pistols into the air and set off firecrackers, and when finally they rode off, they left behind a wake of hope that lingered for days on the air, like the splendid memory of a comet's tail. Soon the Colonel was the favourite. No one had ever witnessed such a phenomenon: a man who surfaced from the civil war, covered with scars and speaking like a professor, a man whose fame spread to every corner of the land and captured the nation's heart. The press focused their attention on him. Newspapermen came from far away to interview him and repeat his phrases, and the number of his followers and enemies continued to grow.

'We're doing great, Colonel,' said El Mulato, after twelve successful weeks of campaigning.

But the Candidate did not hear. He was repeating his secret words, as he did more and more obsessively. He said them when he was mellow with nostalgia; he murmured them in his sleep; he carried them with him on horseback; he thought them before delivering his famous speech; and he caught himself savouring them in his leisure time. And every time he thought of those two words, he thought of Belisa Crepusculario, and his senses were inflamed with the memory of her feral scent, her fiery heat, the whisper of her hair and her sweet mint breath in his ear, until he began to go around like a sleepwalker, and his men realised that he might die before he ever sat in the presidential chair.

'What's got hold of you, Colonel,' El Mulato asked so often that finally one day his chief broke down and told him the source of his befuddlement: those two words that were buried like two daggers in his gut.

'Tell me what they are and maybe they'll lose their magic,' his faithful aide suggested.

'I can't tell them, they're for me alone,' the Colonel replied.

Saddened by watching his chief decline like a man with a death sentence on his head, El Mulato slung his rifle over his shoulder and set out to find Belisa Crepusculario. He followed her trail through all that vast country, until he found her in a village in the far south, sitting under her tent reciting her rosary of news. He planted himself, straddle-legged, before her, weapon in hand.

'You! You're coming with me,' he ordered.

She had been waiting. She picked up her inkwell, folded the canvas of her small stall, arranged her shawl around her shoulders, and without a word took her place behind El Mulato's saddle. They did not exchange so much as a word in all the trip; El Mulato's desire for her had turned into rage, and only his fear of her tongue prevented his cutting her to shreds with his whip. Nor was he inclined to tell her that the Colonel was in a fog, and that a spell whispered into his ear had done what years of battle had not been able to do. Three days later they arrived at the encampment, and immediately, in view of all the troops, El Mulato led his prisoner before the Candidate.

'I brought this witch here so you can give her back her words, Colonel,' El Mulato said, pointing the barrel of his rifle at the woman's head. 'And then she can give you back your manhood.'

The Colonel and Belisa Crepusculario stared at each other, measuring one another from a distance. The men knew then that their leader would never undo the witchcraft of those two accursed words, because the whole world could see the voracious puma's eyes soften as the woman walked to him and took his hand in hers.

OLIVER'S EVOLUTION

JOHN UPDIKE

> **John Updike** (1932-2009) was an American writer who wrote more than twenty novels and published many collections of short stories. He is one of the few writers to have won the Pulitzer Prize for fiction more than once.
>
> 'Oliver's Evolution' was written for *Esquire Magazine* in 1998.
>
> At 650 words long, it's an example of 'flash fiction' – a very short story.

His parents had not meant to abuse him; they had meant to love him, and did love him. But Oliver had come late in their little pack of offspring, at a time when the challenge of child-rearing was wearing thin, and he proved susceptible to mishaps. A big foetus, cramped in his mother's womb, he was born with in-turned feet, and learned to crawl with corrective casts up to his ankles. When they were at last removed, he cried in terror, because he thought those heavy plaster boots scraping and bumping along the floor had been part of himself.

One day in his infancy they found him on their dressing-room floor with a box of mothballs, some of which were wet with saliva; in retrospect they wondered if there had really been a need to rush him to the hospital and have his poor little stomach pumped. His face was grey-green afterwards. The following summer, when he had learned to walk, his parents had unthinkingly swum away off the beach together, striving for romantic harmony the morning after a late party and an alcoholic quarrel, and were quite unaware, until they saw the lifeguard racing along the beach, that Oliver had toddled after them and had been floating on his face for what might have been, given a less alert lifeguard, a fatal couple of minutes. This time, his face was blue, and he coughed for hours.

He was the least complaining of their children. He did not blame his parents when neither they nor the school authorities detected his 'sleepy' right eye in time for therapy, with the result that when he closed that eye everything looked intractably fuzzy. Just the sight of the boy holding a schoolbook at a curious angle to the light made his father want to weep, impotently.

And it happened that he was just the wrong, vulnerable age when his parents went through their separation and divorce. His older brothers were off in boarding school and college, embarked on manhood, free of family. His younger sister was small enough to find the new arrangements – the meals in restaurants with her father, the friendly men who appeared to take her mother out – exciting. But Oliver, at thirteen, felt the weight of the household descend on him; he made his mother's sense of abandonment his own. Again, his father impotently grieved. It was he, and not the boy, who was at fault, really, when the bad grades began to come in from day school, and then from college, and Oliver broke his arm falling down the frat stairs, or leaping, by another account of the confused incident, from a girl's dormitory window. Not one but several family automobiles met a ruinous end with him at the wheel, though with no more injury, as it happened, than contused knees and loosened front teeth. The teeth grew firm again, thank God, for his innocent smile, slowly spreading across his face as the full humour of his newest misadventure dawned, was one of his best features. His teeth were small and round and widely spaced – baby teeth. ■

Then he married, which seemed yet another mishap, to go with the late nights, abandoned jobs, and fallen-through opportunities of his life as a young adult. The girl, Alicia, was as accident-prone as he, given to substance abuse and unwanted pregnancies. Her emotional disturbances left herself and others bruised. By comparison, Oliver was solid and surefooted, and she looked up to him. This was the key. What we expect of others, they endeavour to provide. He held on to a job, and she held on to her pregnancies. You should see him now, with their two children, a fair little girl and a dark-haired boy. Oliver has grown broad, and holds the two of them at once. They are birds in a nest. He is a tree, a sheltering boulder. He is a protector of the weak.

DOG, CAT, AND BABY

JOE R. LANSDALE

> **Joe R. Lansdale** (1951-) is an American writer who has published 43 novels and short stories in many genres, including horror and science fiction. He has also written for comics. Much of his writing has a dark humour and features the strange and the absurd, such an aging Elvis Presley battling an Egyptian mummy in an old people's home, as seen in *Bubba Ho-Tep*.
>
> This story was first published in 1999.

Dog did not like Baby. For that matter, Dog did not like Cat. But Cat had claws – sharp claws.

Dog had always gotten attention. Pat on head. 'Here, boy, here's a treat. Nice dog. Good dog. Shake hands. Speak! Sit. Nice dog.'

Now there was Baby.

Cat had not been a problem, really.

Cat was liked, not loved by family. They petted Cat sometimes. Fed her. Did not mistreat her. But they did not love her. Not way they loved Dog – before Baby.

Damn little pink thing that cried.

Baby got 'Oooohs and Ahhhs.' When Dog tried to get close to Masters, they say, 'Get back, boy. Not *now*.'

When would it be *now*?

Dog never see now. Always Baby get now. Dog get nothing. Sometimes they so busy with Baby it be all day before Dog get fed. Dog never gets treats anymore. Could not remember last pat on head or 'Good Dog!'

Bad business. Dog not like it. ▌

Dog decide to do something about it.

Kill Baby. Then there be Dog, Cat again. They not love Cat, so things be okay.

Dog thought that over. Wouldn't take much to rip little Baby apart. Baby soft, pink. Would bleed easy.

Baby often put in Jumper that hung between doorway when Master Lady hung wash. Baby be easy to get then.

So Dog waited.

One day Baby put in Jumper and Master Lady go outside to hang wash. Dog looks at pink thing jumping, thinks about ripping to pieces. Thinks on it long and hard. Thought makes him so happy his mouth drips water. Dog starts toward Baby, making fine moment last.

Baby looks up, sees Dog coming toward it slowly, almost creeping. Baby starts to cry. ▌

But before Dog can reach Baby, Cat jumps.

Cat been hiding behind couch.

Cat goes after Dog, tears Dog's face with teeth, with claws. Dog bleeds, tries to run. Cat goes after him.

Dog turns to bite.

Cat hangs claw in Dog's eye.

Dog yelps, runs.

Cat jumps on Dog's back, biting Dog on top of head.

Dog tries to turn corner into bedroom. Cat, tearing at him with claws, biting with teeth, makes Dog lose balance. Dog running very fast, fast as he can go, hits the edge of doorway, stumbles back, falls over.

Cat gets off Dog.

Dog lies still.

Dog not breathing.

Cat knows Dog is dead. Cat licks blood from claws, from teeth with rough tongue.

Cat has gotten rid of Dog.

Cat turns to look down hall where Baby is screaming.

Now for *other* one.

Cat begins to creep down hall.

THE GULF

GERALDINE MCCAUGHREAN

> **Geraldine McCaughrean** (1951-) says that her motto is 'Do not write about what you know, write about what you want to know.' She is perhaps best known for her novel *The Kite Rider,* chosen by the Booktrust as one of the 100 Best Books for 12-14 year olds. 'The Gulf' was first published in 1999.

The cold, thin air in the back of his throat was like swallowing swords, but he ran until sweat burst through his skin, until the sweat dried to salt. He ran until every searchlight, floodlight and white-winking barrack window was out of sight and he was running in utter darkness. He ran until night gave way to morning, and every moment he expected to hear shouts or motors or the barking of dogs on his trail.

With sunrise he allowed his hopes to rise too, like a hot, orange ball of flame within his chest. Might he after all make good his escape? Might he reach safety, against all the odds? No one ever did, they had told him. No one ever would. But the hope kept rising in his throat until it buckled his mouth into a smile.

Then he reached the gulf.

He almost ran straight into it – a gorge of such dizzying depth that the river in the bottom was only a green thread; a canyon so wide that a horse at full gallop could not have leapt even halfway across. And its sides were sheer.

Juan fell to his knees, grazing his forehead on the bark of a dead, fallen tree, his arms over his head. Had he come this far to meet disappointment like a snake across his path? There was no way over. The gulf stretched as far as the eye could see to right and left. He could leap into it or wait at the brink for his pursuers to catch up with him. But he was done for. It was true. No one ever escaped. No one ever would.

When he raised his head, Juan saw a little girl watching him. She stood on the far side of the canyon, rubbing a twist of grass between her hands. 'Want to cross over?' she said. In the silence of the empty landscape her voice floated easily over to him. She did not have to shout.

She spoke the dialect of the neighbouring country. The river gorge must be the border, then. Juan had reached the border – a stone's throw from safety. 'Is there a bridge? Anywhere? A bridge?' he called.

'No. No bridge... But I could fetch my sisters.' She put her fingers in her mouth and whistled shrilly.' Juan gave a laugh somewhere between a bark and a sob. Much good her sisters would do him.

The girls came dawdling out from the long grass and regarded him with the same solemn brown eyes. Each was rubbing a twist of grass between her hands.

'He wants to cross over,' said the sister.

'Better tell the brothers,' they said.

Ten boys emerged from the swashing grass, carrying sickles and armfuls of grass. They sat.

Down on the far side of the ravine, dangling their legs over the rim, their hands began to work in that same nervous, habitual motion, rubbing the grass stems together into long tasseled cords.

'Go home,' said Juan, glancing over his shoulder. He did not want them to witness either his tears or his recapture. He had no idea how much of a lead he had gained on his pursuers. Eight hours? Nine?

'They chasing you?' called one of the boys, swatting flies.

'I thought I could reach the border. But the gulf … I didn't know …'

Their sunburned faces expressed no sympathy, no sadness at this predicament. Their small worn hands just went on twisting grass.

'I'll tell the mothers,' said the littlest boy, and ran off, his bare feet unsettling flies in clouds.

Literary Shorts – An Anthology

The village must have been just over the ridge, for he soon returned, towing his mother by the hand. For the first time, Juan realised that the grass-twirling was not a nervous habit but a livelihood. The mothers – handsome women with shining plaits to which their babies clung – were also twirling the grass together into fibres, their big hands worn horny by the coarse stems. They contemplated Juan with large, dark-fringed eyes. 'You need help,' said one.

Juan laughed hollowly. 'I am past helping. This gulf did for me.'

The women called the children together, took their cords of grass, and began, simply by rubbing, to splice the thin lengths into thicker, longer ones. 'Fetch the grandmas and grandpas,' they told the littlest boy.

Away he went, and fetched back with him the old people of the village – mumbling, bent, bone-weary old bodies who shook their heads and clutched their shawls round them, even though the day was hot. One old matriarch, her hat as big as a bundle of laundry, flumped down amid her skirts, and the women laid their grass-cords at her feet, as if paying homage. Her whispering palms twirled their individual cords into one long rope, with a deftness which defied belief. For a few blessed minutes Juan watched with such intent fascination that he forgot his own peril and strained to make out what magical process, what cunning craftsmanship, could twist grass into rope.

Then, with a jolt of hope sharp as a kick, he realised that the rope was for him – to get him over the ravine.

What well-meaning, simple fools! Inwardly he raged with bitter laughter. Even if they succeeded in making a cable strong enough to carry the weight of a man, long enough to span the gulf, how would they get the end across to him? Impossible! So much work and for what? Around him the evening breeze sprang up, and Juan found he had sat all day by the gulf watching the children and grandparents and mothers opposite labour over the rope, which now lay coiled at the old woman's feet.

That same breeze carried on it the sound of jeep engines, of sirens, of his pursuers.

'What's the point? What's the point?' he bawled, and his voice dropped into the ravine like a rock fall.

The little girl – the one he had seen first – lifted up a coil of the immense rope to show him. It was all she could do to raise it off the ground. 'Father will help,' she said. 'He is coming soon.'

It reduced him to tears – this little mite's touching, ridiculous trust in her father. What would he prove to be, after all, but yet another pigeon-chested peasant in a straw hat, chewing betel nuts and hoping for a quiet life. A man like Juan.

The little girl's father proved, however, to be a big, energetic man – a hunter. When he arrived, his jeans and shirt dusty after a day on the plateau, he found the village assembled by the ravine, saw Juan, saw the rope, and instantly re-strung his bow. His grandmother threaded a needle with sewing thread, and stuck it through the grass rope, then gave the thread to her grandson. He tied it to his arrow and, without a word to Juan… fired it straight at him.

The arrow gouged up the soil between Juan's feet. With trembling fingers, he snatched the cotton, winding the loops so tight round his hand that his fingers went blue. The rope was heavy, but the sewing thread did not break. Like a great anaconda, the rope's end sagged its way across the ravine, and Juan made it fast around the log. The strongest of the villagers took hold of the other end and braced themselves.

The jeeps were visible now, bouncing over the rough terrain, the evening sun flashing on their windscreens. In the normal way of things, Juan could never have brought himself to do what he did next. But after so many people had done so much, he could hardly hesitate. Hanging like a tree sloth under the grass rope he crabbed his way over the yawning, heart-numbing terror of the vertiginous drop, fixing all his thoughts on the beauty of the hawser, the thousand different shades of yellow and green all interwoven into one speckled cable. How could something so strong be made of such frail component parts? The seed-dust made him sneeze.

The jeeps skidded to a halt just as hands – old and young and callused – closed in Juan's hair and round his arms and through his belt and pulled him to safety. Then the villagers dropped their end of the great rope into the ravine. It thumped against the far wall, shedding a shower of seeds.

Juan jumped to his feet and shook a defiant fist at the men on the opposite bank. In his raised hand was a single twist of grass.

THE PARADISE CARPET

JAMILA GAVIN

Jamila Gavin (1941-) was born in India, to an English mother and an Indian father. She has written many novels for children, perhaps her best known being *Coram Boy*, a children's historical novel about Toby, saved from an African slave ship, and Aaron, the illegitimate son of the heir to a great estate.

'The Paradise Carpet' was first published in 2002.

'One knot blue, two knots yellow, three knots red, four knots green... The young boys chanted the pattern of the carpet they were weaving. Bony little fingers deftly drew the card down the thread; warp and weft... warp and weft... top to bottom, right to left... warp and weft and knot.

Behind the loom inside a dark mud hut, crouching like caged animals, sat a line of boys. With backs against a wall, their thin arms rose and fell as they drew the threads from top to bottom, right to left, warp and weft and knot. They could have been musicians plucking at strings, but these were carpet weavers whose harmonies were of the eye not the ear as, bit by bit, the glorious patterns and hues of a rich carpet emerged in the darkness. 'One knot blue, two knots yellow, three knots red, four knots green ...' The boys wove their thread, prompted and guided by old Rama, the only man among them, who had the pattern pinned to an upright in front of him.

II

'Ishwar, you're dreaming again!' bellowed a harsh voice. THWACK! The hand of the overseer struck a boy around the head.

The boy, Ishwar, faltered and nearly fell over sideways but Bharat, crouching next to him, braced his body and managed to keep his friend upright.

'Keep your mind on the job. There'll be no supper for any of you tonight until you've woven another ten inches,' threatened the man. His great shape filled the doorway and blotted out their only source of light. Then he was gone. There was low groan from the boys. Another ten inches before they would eat! That could take two hours or more, for this was the most complicated carpet they had ever woven – and the whole thing was to be completed within seven months – when an ordinary carpet took at least twelve.

A wealthy man had come along the rough track to the village in his white Mercedes. When he reached the brick house of Anoup, the carpet manufacturer, he got out like a raja, surrounded by shy jostling children and deferential elders, all of whom noted the gold rings embedded in his chubby fingers, and the chunky foreign watch just glinting beneath the cuffs of his smart suit.

'I want a carpet for my daughter's dowry,' he declared. 'She is to be married next December.' (Everyone did an instant calculation. That was only seven months away.) 'And this is the pattern I want you to weave.'

Anoup took the piece of paper the rich man held out to him. He stared at it long and silently, then gloomily and apologetically shook his head. 'Impossible,' he said. 'I need at least twelve months to do an average carpet – but this... this... and in SEVEN months, you say... No. Impossible.'

The rich man pulled out a fat briefcase from the car. He opened it up. There was a gasp from the onlookers. No one had ever seen so much money. Great wads of it, all stapled and bound straight from the bank. 'This is what you get now – and the rest when its finished. I'm sure you can do it. Just work a little harder – and a little longer each day, eh?' He tweaked the ear of the nearest little boy.

'I... er...' Anoup hesitated.

'Take it, take it...' voices around him urged.

Anoup's brain spun. Common sense said, don't do it... you can't do it... But the money... 'I'll do it. Your carpet will be ready on time.'

Anoup gave old Rama the pattern. 'You'd better study this,' he said.

Now Rama knew why Anoup had hesitated. The pattern was a paradise garden of strutting peacocks with sweeping tails, gold spotted deer leaping through undergrowth, squirrels coiling round tree-trunks and monkeys swinging from bough to bough; all sorts of exotic birds swooped and trilled and pecked at luscious fruit and flowers. Most extraordinary of all, was the Tree of Life, from its spreading roots at the base, rising up and up through twisting coiling branches, all the way to the top where the rays of rising sun pierced golden shafts through the leaves. It would need thread of every colour in the rainbow. 'There aren't enough hours in the day...' Rama protested softly.

'Then we will use the hours of the night too,' Anoup retorted harshly.

Ishwar stared at the bright blue square in the doorway – the blue of the sky outside. He longed to leap up and charge into the daylight and play, play, play. He had almost forgotten what the outside was like. It was two years since his mother had brought him to this village to be bonded to Anoup, for debts incurred in his grandfather's lifetime. Since then he had worked behind a loom in the dark, airless mud hut. It was like that for all of them; bonded and enslaved – even old Rama – and Ishwar knew he too would die in bondage, that the debt would never be paid off in his lifetime either.

Ishwar could hear the voices of the village children being taught under the neem tree to chorus out their times tables and their alphabet. Ishwar tried to listen and learn – but it was no use. He must chant for ever with the other carpet weavers, the colours of the thread they were weaving... one knot yellow, two knots blue, three knots red, four knots green...

The paradise garden shimmered on the loom. If he couldn't play outside, then he must roam within its green shade and splash in the stream and chase the deer and climb branch by branch up and up the Tree of Life until he reached the blue sky there on the loom. With a strange eagerness, he took up the thread and moved his card top to bottom, right to left, warp and weft and knot, as if he would weave himself into the carpet. ∎

Exactly when the seven months were over, the white Mercedes came. The villagers watched anxiously as the rich man came as before, right up to Anoup's door.

'Is it ready?'

'It is,' answered Anoup, eyeing the bulging briefcase on the back seat.

'Show it to me. You realise that if it is not exactly what I ordered, I will not take it.'

'Sir, it is exactly what you asked for in every detail,' boasted Anoup.

'I'll be the judge of that,' snorted the rich man. 'Bring it out in the daylight where I can examine it properly.'

Anoup clicked his fingers. Rama and three boys ran to the hut.

'Hey, Ishwar!' exclaimed Rama. 'Wake up, boy! Help us with the carpet.'

Ishwar was sitting in his usual place behind the loom, his head leaning against the upright. He didn't respond.

'Hurry up!' bellowed Anoup impatiently. Rama and the boys lugged the carpet outside and with almost holy reverence, unrolled it. Even the villagers gasped in amazement at the beauty and workmanship. It was a miracle. They beamed with pride.

The rich man came forward till his nose nearly touched the pile. Inch by inch he scrutinised the carpet. Suddenly, he roared with fury. 'What's this!' he shouted. 'I didn't ask for this! What kind of idiotic thing have you done here! I can't take it – not with THIS!' He dragged the carpet out of their hands and trampled it into the dust. Then leaving the villagers appalled and stunned the rich businessman got into his car and sped off at top speed.

Nobody moved. Fearful eyes turned to Anoup. He was standing as if turned to stone. At last he clicked his fingers. In horrified silence they held out the carpet. Anoup's expert eye began at the tip and scanned the carpet, as he had done twenty times each day. In his mind's eye, he wove each thread himself. He panned along the twisting branches of the Tree of Life, the glowing colours of humming birds and nightingales, dropping down through ten shades of green leaves and a dozen shades of blossoms of red, pink, purple and violet; he noted the golden fur of a deer darting through the grass, the hundred eyes of a peacock's tail shimmering near a silver fountain... and...?

Then Anoup's body shuddered. He shuddered so hard, they heard his teeth rattle, and the bones of his fingers clicking as he ground his knuckles into his fist.

'What is it?' murmured the villagers. 'What has he seen?' They surged forward. Speechless with rage, Anoup pointed to a spot deep in the undergrowth. Almost hidden among blossom and foliage, the young face of a boy peered up at the Tree of Life, an arm upstretched, ready to climb.

'Ishwar!' Rama muttered under his breath. 'It's Ishwar!'

'Ishwar!' The name was shrieked in vengeance! The villagers rushed to the hut.

The boy still leaned against the loom as if resting his aching head. Anoup strode over and kicked him. The boy slipped forward, face down, on to the earth floor. When they rolled him over, they saw he was dead.

RESIGNED

MEG ROSOFF

> **Meg Rosoff** (1956-) is an American writer, based in London. Best known for her young-adult novel, *How I Live Now*, which came out as a film in 2013, her work centres round the complex emotions and relationships present in young people's lives. 'Resigned', first published in 2011, is an excellent example of how her work tries to capture the experience of being a teenager.

My Mother has resigned.

Not from her job, but from being a mother. ‖ She said she'd had enough, more than enough. In actual fact, she used what my dad calls certain good old-fashioned Anglo-Saxon words that they're allowed to use and we're not. She said we could bring ourselves up from now on, she wanted no more part in it.

She said what she did all day was the laundry, the cooking, the shopping, the cleaning, the making the beds, the clearing the table, the packing and unpacking the dish-washer, the dragging everyone to ballet and piano and cello and football and swimming, not to mention school, the shouting at everyone to get ready, the making sure everyone had the right kit for the right event, the making cakes for school cake sales, the helping with homework, the making the garden look nice, the feeding the fish we couldn't be bothered to feed, the walking the dog we'd begged to have and then ignored, the making packed lunches for school according to what we would and wouldn't eat (for those of us who have packed lunches) and then the unmaking them after school with all the things we didn't eat, the remembering dinner money (for those of us who didn't want packed lunches), and not to mention, she said, all the nagging in between.

Here she paused, which was good because we all thought the strain of talking so fast without stopping was going to make her pass out. But quick as a flash she was off again. Dad stood grinning in the corner, by the way, like all this had nothing at all to do with him, but we knew it was just a matter of time before she remembered she was married and then the you-know-what was going to hit the you-know-who.

Mum took a deep breath.

And another thing.

She had her fingers out for this one. And there weren't enough fingers in the room to list the next set of crimes.

Who did we think took care of the bank accounts, the car insurance, the life insurance, the mortgage, the tax returns, the milk bill, the charity donations, the accountant...

Here she paused again, looking around the kitchen to make absolutely certain she had our full attention and eye contact and no one was thinking of escape – even for a minute or two – from the full force of her resentment.

II

We are not totally stupid, by the way. We read the tabloids often enough to know that between a mother giving a lecture of the fanatical nervous breakdown variety to her kids and Grievous Bodily Harm there is a very fine line indeed. *The Sun*, for instance, seems to specialise in stories along the lines of *Formerly average mum bludgeons family with stern lecture and tyre iron, then makes cup of tea*. We three kids were doing the eye contact and respectful hangdog-look thing, maintaining that pathetic silence that makes mothers feel guilty eventually, when they're done shouting. But we had to give the old girl credit, this time she showed no sign of flagging.

She took another deep breath.

... the magazine subscriptions, the dentist appointments, the birthday parties, the Christmas dinner, the presents, the nephews and nieces, the *in-laws*.

As one, we swivelled to look at Dad. Mum had stopped and was looking at Dad too, whose brain you could tell was racing with possible escape routes, excuses, mitigating circumstances, and of course the desire to be somewhere else entirely. He shot a single furtive glance at the back door, figured it was too far to risk making a break for it. (Mum is no slouch in the lunge-and-tackle stakes, having been a county champion lacrosse player back a hundred years ago when she was in school. We knew she hadn't forgotten all the moves due to an incident a few years ago with an attempted purse-snatching. None of us refers to it now, but word on the street is that the guy still never leaves the house.)

And, she said (glaring at me because the woman is an experienced enough mother to hear you thinking a digression about lacrosse), *and* I hope you are listening, because when I say *I am not going to do it anymore*, I mean I am not going to do it anymore. She glared at each one of us in turn – a kind of equal-opportunity glare.

And one last thing, she said, in an even scarier, quieter voice, and I risked a sideways glance to see if Francis Ford Coppola was in the wings directing this masterful performance. *From this moment on*, she continued, I am deaf to whining. Deaf to any annoying tone of voice *you three* – she shot a relatively benign look at Dad just to let him know he was off the hook on this particular issue, assuming he backed her up, that is – *can dream up*. Screaming will only be acknowledged if accompanied by bones sticking out of skin or hatchet actually *buried* in skull.

Moe was shuffling his feet a little now, and sneaking peeks at his watch because his teacher hated it when anyone was late to school.

She glared at him and he jumped to attention like someone out of the Queen's Guard.

Right, she said, surveying her troops and appearing a little calmer now. Any questions?

Nobody dared say anything, except, of course, Alec, who could smarm for England and has not lived fifteen years on this earth without picking up a trick or two along the way. He had stopped lounging against the wall, which is what he does with most of his waking hours, stood up fairly straight, plastered this sickening look of sincerity across his wily mug and said, OK, Mum, fair cop, we're with you on this. I'm only surprised you didn't make a stand a long time ago.

Then, just to prove she wasn't born yesterday either, Mum made this kind of snorting sound and rolled her eyes, indicating rejection of smarm, and said, I can't tell you how pleased I am that you approve, Alec. Now everyone better get a move on because school starts in twenty minutes and you are going to have to figure out how to get there.

As one, we turned to Dad, who was now trying to make himself two-dimensional and slide behind the fridge, which would have been easier if he hadn't been six-foot-four and built like a rugby scrum half. But Dad is a man who knows when to fold in poker, like when all he's got in his hand are twos, threes, and fours of different colours. He folded gracefully.

Come on then, he said in a resigned voice. Pile in. We'll leave Mum alone for now and give her some time to collect herself.

Some time to collect myself? Mum said. *Some* time *to collect myself*? How kind, how fantastically kind of you. Why, I can't think *how* to show my appreciation short of taking out a full-page ad in the *effing Financial Times*. (She practically screamed that last bit.) But, say what you will. I now have *the rest of my life* to myself, and it's you suckers who are going to have to cope.

She smiled at us then, a genuine smile, all warm and mumsy and loving, and kissed us each in turn, the way you'd kiss people who were trooping off to a firing squad.

Have a lovely day, all of you. See you later.

We hated it when she turned all nice and snatched the moral high ground out from under us. But it was getting late so we all crammed into Dad's car, elbowing and kicking and biting each other like captives in a government crocodile-breeding initiative, and headed off to be late to school.

Naturally there was a fair bit of conversation in the car about Mum's little episode.

She's bluffing, Alec said. She's probably just getting her period.

I wouldn't be so sure, smart-arse, Dad said. She didn't look like she was bluffing to me. And just a tip for later life – don't ever even *think* those words in the vicinity of a woman or you'll find yourself castrated before you can say oops.

Moe grinned and I sniggered, knowing our dear big brother's future was definitely going to be bollock-free.

Anyway, we got to school late, and all of us got detention, except Moe, who has a professional way of looking like he's about to burst into tears. By lunchtime we'd all forgotten that we even had a mum at home, what with all the gossip and sexual harassment and who's not talking to who and have you noticed who *she's* hanging around with these days to talk about.

After school, Moe and I caught a ride home with Esther's mum, who wears flowery clothes and acts like a proper mum, asking if you're hungry and doling out crisps and having tissues with her at all times, and never screaming *shut* the bloody **** up! at her children like someone else I can think of. Not that I'd want her as my mum, due to her being an irony-free zone, not to mention harbouring a fervent wish for Esther to grow up to be a Person of Substance, an expression she actually uses in public, which explains why Esther looks so long-suffering and wants to be a flight attendant.

My mum always said she wanted me to be a ballerina, which is her idea of the world's funniest joke because I'm not exactly small and could be two ballerinas if they cut me in half and I had four legs. Moe wants to be a vet, like every other eight-year-old, and Alec just wants to get out of school, drink alcohol, go clubbing, get his driver's license, get a car, and have a girlfriend who'll let him have sex with her all the time, though not necessarily in that order.

But I'm getting off the point here.

We stayed at Esther's for supper, dutifully notifying Mum so she couldn't shout that she'd gone to all the trouble to make us a nice blah blah blah with three kinds of blah blah blah on the side and we weren't there to eat it and hadn't even had the courtesy to phone.

She seemed pleased to hear that we weren't coming home for dinner, and it wasn't until I hung up that I realised she hadn't said the usual – if you're not home by seven, you're toast – but I took it as tacit and made sure Esther's mum gave us a ride home. We walked in the door at ten to seven, which I thought was a pretty good touch, just in case someone's watch might be running a few minutes fast.

Mum was on the phone when we got there, talking to her business partner, Jo. They'd had a lot of interest from America after the article that was written about them in *Country Life*, and apparently antique garden implements were all the rage among rich Americans who had too much money and not enough antique garden implements.

I noticed immediately that the breakfast table looked exactly the same as it had when we all left for school that morning, with dirty dishes and open jars of marmalade and crumbs everywhere, and I thought Mum was going a bit far to prove a point, given how much she hates mess of any kind, but I thought I'd better play along and so started clearing up. I shouted for Alec to come help, but he said he didn't give a monkey's whether it was cleared up or not, and since we were in charge we should be able to live in squalor if squalor was what we liked.

As squalor went, this was pretty tame, and anyway I had homework to do and got distracted by Hooligan wanting to go out for a walk and since Mum wasn't giving orders anymore, I let him out in the garden and even he looked confused that no one was shouting at him to stay away from the herbaceous borders.

Hey, Moe, I hissed. Get this. And I pointed to Hoo out in the garden doing a poo the size of Mont-Saint-Michel by Mum's *Nicotiana sylvestris*, and Moe's eyes widened and we both thought, cool!

After that we forgot about Hoo and watched some television while pretending to do homework and in the commercial breaks I managed to write a whole essay entitled 'The Egyptians: Why They Became Extinct'.

After the initial shock, this new regime was turning out to be much more relaxing than life with Mussolini. Oops, did I say a fanatic Italian dictator? I meant Mum.

When Dad finally got home he looked a little grumpy about no dinner being on the table, but it wasn't long till he got the hang of things and filled a soup bowl full of Frosties and sighed really loud a few times to make sure everyone knew he wasn't thrilled about the new order. Moe looked at Dad's Frosties and, because no one said no, he had some too.

Over the next week or so, Mum moved into her office in the garden, which she'd had the foresight to make Dad build with its own shower room and enough of a kitchen to survive on. Also, as she put it, there was no way she was going to step foot in the kitchen until we four called pest control. She still came to say good night to us, a little like a fond auntie, and sometimes we hung around and did our homework in her office because every place in the whole house seemed to have something messing up the surfaces where you might want to put a book. And she didn't seem to mind us coming in as long as we didn't bother her or leave wrappers on the floor. Which was tricky, given that all our meals seemed to come in wrappers these days. She was on the phone a lot, and having meetings with her partner and smiling more than we'd seen in ages.

Which was great.

Only, after a few weeks of this, us kids were starting to look at each other and think, hey, fun's fun, but there are no clean clothes in the whole house and we've run out of cereal for breakfast and tea, and speaking of tea, there's only one manky box of teabags that came free from Tesco about a hundred years ago and Dad's taken to drinking instant coffee, which puts him in an even worse mood than he is naturally. Also, the dog needs brushing, the radiators make a horrible noise, and every envelope that arrives has *For Your Urgent Attention* written on it in red.

So we sat down that Saturday at what had once been the breakfast table but now looked like that exhibit at the zoo, filled with half-eaten meals and *Rattus norvegicus* probably written on a brass plaque somewhere. I noticed the two goldfish in the bowl on top of the fridge for the first time in ages, and it was clear no one else had noticed them either, considering that they had given up swimming some time ago and taken up floating on the surface. Moe was wearing the cleanest of his shirts, which had ketchup spilled down the front and a chip actually stuck to it, Dad had gone out to have breakfast alone with the newspaper at Starbucks, and Alec and I were drinking blueberry cordial, which was the only thing left to drink in the house since we ran out of teabags and the milkman stopped coming.

OK, guys, I said. I think it's time to start begging.

Moe looked annoyed. But we're doing perfectly well without any help, he said, digging into a bowl of recently thawed peas from the freezer with some week-old takeaway curry mixed in.

Alec said he was going to be sick and Moe should be taken into care, and they began to shout at each other and Alec stormed out, but I called him back because it was so obvious to all of us that something had to be done. We managed to be civil to each other long enough to write a letter setting out our terms of surrender. Here's what we wrote:

Dearest Mum,

You were right. Even we can't live with ourselves.

If you agree to come back we will follow any rules you make with absolutely no complaining and no whining.

Promise. Cross our hearts and hope to die.

Please. We miss you so much.

Plus, we were wrong.

Love,

Your children

I typed the letter up on Dad's laptop, set it in a nice curly font, and after I printed it out we all signed it and drew hearts on it and so forth to suck up, and then we slipped it under the door of the studio and went back into the house and got to work.

It took all day, so it wasn't a bad thing that we didn't hear back from her right away. We scrubbed the floors and the walls, the kitchen and the bathroom, we swept off all the junk piled on every surface and separated out the bills and left them neatly stacked, and Dad paid them when he got home. Moe cleaned out the refrigerator and Alec and I went up to the shop with a lifetime's supply of pocket money and bought food – not the stuff we'd been eating all month, like chocolate breakfast bars, but proper food, like chicken parts and green beans and granary bread and cheddar cheese. We cleaned out the fishbowl and flushed both the fish down the toilet, which wasn't inhumane considering their advanced state of fatality, put clean sheets on all the beds and did about fifteen loads of laundry, and even folded it up afterwards. Alec got out the Hoover, but miracles have to end somewhere, and when the phone rang and it was his girlfriend, I ended up doing it myself.

It was a not entirely unsatisfying day, if I say so myself. Even the house itself seemed less bad-tempered, like it preferred being clean.

Well, Mum may have suspected something was up when she saw all the black rubbish bags stacked outside by the front door, or she might just have got tired of sleeping on the little daybed in the studio. Or maybe she even missed us. Who knows.

But that night, around ten p.m., we saw lights on in the studio, and later found a handwritten note pushed through the letter box.

It read, I'll think about it. Love, Mum.

And I guess she thought about it all day Sunday, because it was teatime on Sunday when she finally knocked on the door like a visitor, and when we let her in, she looked around in every room, and nodded every now and then, and finally she sat down at the (immaculate) kitchen table and said, OK, I'll come back.

We all started cheering and surrounded her and hugged and kissed her, but she held up one hand and continued.

On one condition. At which point she pulled out a sheaf of papers that looked a little like the Treaty of Versailles, and handed one set to each of us, and on it was a schedule of who did what job on what day and, to be fair, she had written herself into the list occasionally too.

So this is where I'm supposed to say we all lived happily ever after, but in fact we didn't – at least, not quite in the way we expected to. ❚❚ Nobody really stuck to the jobs listed on the piece of paper, including Mum, because she was away a lot suddenly due to her business being so successful at last, but the good thing was she seemed to care a lot less about the house being as clean as it was before, and we learned one important lesson – not to push her past a certain point – so we did pitch in more than we ever had, with the possible exception of Alec. Then Mum really started raking in the dough and Dad quit his job and stayed home, doing most of the cooking and cleaning and gardening and seeming strangely happy about it. So in general, things worked out more or less peacefully for a while.

But a few months later, we noticed Mum was spending a lot of time talking to the young guy next door, and one day she gathered us together and said she was moving out for good. We just stood there stunned and completely freaked out, and Moe began to cry, and Mum grabbed him up in her arms and said stop crying, Moe, and come look at my new house.

Then she opened the front door, and jumped over the little wall by the front path and pulled a key out of her pocket and opened the door of the house next door. And while we were staring at her trying to figure out what had happened, she was grinning ear to ear and said I've finally sorted it.

So that's the end of the story. Mum bought the house next door from the young guy, and though we have to take our shoes off when we go visit her, she almost never shouts at us anymore, and she never complains about the mess in our house, not ever. And when I get fed up living with Dad or if I can't stand another minute with Moe and Alec, I move in with Mum for a few weeks and we have a great time staying up late and talking and just getting on. And sometimes we rent a movie and make popcorn and invite Mum round to our house to watch it and she stays over, and we make her breakfast in the morning before she goes back to work.

And whenever anyone asks us in a polite concerned voice why we don't live with our mother, we put on mournful faces and sigh and say, Well, she just walked out on us one day, but we're pretty much resigned to it now.

And then we fall about laughing, and go and tell Mum.

HAPPILY EVER AFTER

BARBARA BLEIMAN

> **Barbara Bleiman** (1955-) was born in South Africa but came to England when she was just five years old. Her great-grandfather emigrated from Lithuania, in Eastern Europe, to South Africa in the early 1900s.
>
> Her parents told her many stories about life for her ancestors in their small Jewish communities in Lithuania and Russia and later in their new home in South Africa.
>
> 'Happily Ever After', first published in 2011, is based on one of these tales from a way of life that has long since past.

This is a story that my mother told me, not once but several times, about a young girl called Bella. She was to become my great-aunt in the end but it was a close-run thing. It almost didn't happen and then, finally, it did.

Bella lived in a *shtetl* in Lithuania. She was a Jew, a peasant girl, living in a little village called Gargzdai or Gorzd, depending on who you were, on the edge of the civilised world, next to the Baltic Sea and in hearing distance of a clock that was ticking towards change – oh my God what change! – at the turn of the first decade of the already turned century. But she'd never see it herself, not with her own eyes. She would miss the blood dripping onto the snow and the tearing down of the houses, the cows lowing and the sheep bleating as they burned.

She said her prayers on the Sabbath, over the two tallow candles, and drank the sweet wine. She hid from the boys with their *talleisim*, their prayer shawls, and long curling locks, who laughed at her on their way to the little *shul* that squatted on the hill. She watched them as they walked along the mud track and past the dairy farm. She helped her mother with the washing, pounding it in a bucket with a washing stick, putting it through the wringer, hanging it by the fire to dry. She learnt to cook the simple food they could afford – potato soup, beetroot and swede, dark rye bread and salty fish, smoked on wood or pickled in a barrel. She sat with her sisters, sewing coarse calico cloth and darning woollen stockings, watching her father, with his prayer book, nodding, back and forth, back and forth, muttering the Hebrew prayers she didn't understand. She saw him fling out his arm in temper and bring the pan lid down with a crack when he was angry, so the table shuddered and trembled. She felt his scratchy woollen coat, when he gathered all his children in the wide shelter of his arms, to kiss them and bless them: 'Oh my pride and my joy. May the good Lord care for you and bring you children of your own.' She heard her mother singing Yiddish songs and watched her hitching her skirts to dance to the fiddle and the accordion at Purim or Shavuot and she danced with her sisters, swinging them round and round. She watched at weddings when the bride and groom were lifted in their chairs and the men clapped and sang and the women danced and laughed and the shy young bride looked out through her veil and the proud young man smashed the ritual glass and everyone shouted '*Mazel tov*, good luck, good luck. May you have health and happiness!' She saw her pimply brother becoming a man at his bar mitzvah and her doe-eyed elder sister being betrothed to Pinchas the butcher, who was twenty years older than her and had a face like an unscrubbed potato. She hid scraps of paper to write on and stole stubs of pencils to write with. She woke in the morning when the scrawny cock crowed and went to her bed when the sun slipped down below the roof of the *shul*. In short, she lived a life and she knew of no other.

***

'Who will you marry?' she asked her friend Sarah as they sat under the bilberry tree by the blacksmith's forge.

'Not Schmuly, with his smelly armpits,' said Sarah. 'Pooey Schmuly'. Not Shorty Isaac, the *mohel's* son, who helped his father with the circumcisions. Not Samuel with his knock-knees or Reuben Four-Eyes who was blind as Esra's grey-haired old dog even though he was still only sixteen. Not Rivka's skinny brother, or any of the Krasner boys; not the Milavetz brothers or the five ugly Plotkins, with their mule and their sulky faces. No no no. Not one of them. The girls held their noses and screwed up their faces – yuck – and laughed and laughed. They were fifteen years old and hid behind their mother's skirts when stupid boys came to the door.

And then pretty Sarah was married, just like that, to Avram, the oldest of the Plotkins. Now she had no time to sit under the bilberry tree and laugh at silly boys. She held a raw-faced baby with a runny nose under her arm as she beat the eggs for the fruit pudding, and rocked the wooden cradle with her foot as she twisted hanks of wool or sorted buttons. She was a woman with a woman's cares.

Bella wondered when she would be married and which of the Krazners or Milavetz boys or four ugly Plotkins she should hide from when they came knocking on her father's door. But none of them came and the years went by and Bella's sisters and brothers flew up and grew away and Bella was left at home, spending her evenings watching her father nodding over his prayers and her mother nodding over her knitting.

Then one cold evening, when the ice hung from the eaves and the branches of the lime tree were broken and bowed with heavy snow, there was a knock at the door. It was Moishe, the matchmaker, come with a proposition. Pa and Ma's sleepiness vanished, despite the blackness of the night and the fug of warmth from the fire. They sat up straight as wood.

'I have a match for your daughter. He's a boy, oh my God, what a boy! And what a family! And what an opportunity for the girl, who isn't, let's face it, so young any more.'

Ma opened her mouth and shut it again.

'But where does he live?' asked Ma, hoping for a *shtetl* to the south, so she could borrow a cart and go and visit, whenever she felt like it. Already Ma was thinking of the grandchildren and the *naches*, the joy they would bring, and helping to rock them and wean them and knit their coats and sing them her songs.

'Ah,' said Moishe. 'Ah.' He paused and sighed. 'I'll have that cup of warm milk that you're offering,' he said.

'Not over the hills to the North and Plungė,' said Ma. 'We couldn't accept that.'

'No,' said Moishe. 'Not over the hills to Plungė. But a little way away,' he said, sipping on the warm milk. 'But let's not worry about that for now,' and he proceeded to tell them about the boy, Solomon Schachat, son of Samuel, grandson of Abraham, great-grandson of Chaim, who used to live in the village many, many years earlier. 'A catch,' he said, 'Money, there's plenty! A rich young man, so rich he keeps his money in a bank. She'll be drowning in it. No rough woollen coats for her from now on. Cashmere and silk, she'll be wearing. Pearls and fine jewels. Not the stink of the *shtetl* for her.'

Pa stroked his beard. 'Mmm,' he said. 'Mmm.'

'Here is a photograph,' said Moishe, at which point Bella jumped up from the bottom step where she was sitting and ran over to take a look. She saw a fine-looking young man, with a starched collar and a dark woven suit. He had bright eyes and a hint of a smile, despite the customary formal pose for the photograph.

'Yes,' she said. 'I want him.' And that was that. Pa and Ma shook hands with Moishe, Bella clapped her hands together and spun round the room, as pleased as the cow when she'd just been fed.

'So which village does he live in?' asked Ma, hugging Bella to her.

'Cape Town,' said Moishe quietly and as Ma opened her mouth to scream, 'You must give her this chance,' he said. 'Her whole life will change. She will be rich.'

And so, one early morning, before the cock crowed, or the cow was fed, before Sarah Plotkin had woken to give her fifth son his feed, ▌▌ or the rabbi had woken from his bed to say his early-morning prayers, Bella was climbing into a cart that would take her to a station where she would board a steam train that would take her to Libau, where she would find a man who would escort her to the docks, where she would climb the gangplank onto a steamship, where she would spend three weeks crossing the oceans in the cheapest cabin available, being sick in the washbasin or over the side of the ship or into the bin in the cabin she shared with three other women, of various sizes and smells and dirty habits, who took out their teeth at night, or picked at the snag of a toenail, or left the door open when they sat on the toilet, and where she would wake up one morning and look out from the deck at a ruffle of land, with a flat-topped mountain that looked like a table, which she would watch approaching and feel her stomach heave like curdled milk pudding as she realised that somewhere on that shore was the good-looking young man to whom she would be married, and the house and family that would become her own.

***

A month later and Bella is back on the same steamship, doing her journey in reverse, returning to Libau, back to her ma and pa and Gargzdai. She is standing on the deck watching the flat mountain turn grey and misty and the ruffle of land become a shuddery blur. What can have gone wrong? Before the ship has left the docks at Cape Town, a letter arrives for Sarah Plotkin, the only letter she has ever received in her life, the only one she will ever receive, brought to her by Pooey Schmuly who doubles as the postman when he's not helping his father in the fields. When the littlest Plotkin is off her hands, having his afternoon nap, she takes the letter into the outside shack that stands for a toilet and reads it there, where she knows she will not be disturbed by the rest of her children.

'Oy vay, oy vay,' Sarah whispers to herself as she sits, struggling to read the words in the little beam of light that squeezes through a crack in the wood.

Dearest Sarah,

My letter will come as a surprise. I am coming home. Please tell my ma and pa, so that I don't have to. You will want to know why, so I will tell you and you can weep for me, as I know you will because you are my dear friend.

Sarah reads on, ignoring the cries of her children arguing over their hoop and ball. Then she dries her tears on her apron, folds up the letter, runs into the house, grabs the little ones, puts on their heavy coats one by one and herds them like sheep towards Bella's house at the other side of the village.

When Sarah arrives Bella's parents are lighting candles for the Sabbath.

'She's coming home,' cries Sarah.

When Bella's ma has been revived with a small glass of wine and Bella's pa has stopped swearing and cursing and is finally calm enough to listen, she tells them the story, reading out passages from the letter as she goes.

I was met at the docks by the whole family, all lined up – Solomon, his ma and pa, the five older sisters, their husbands and their children. I knew him straightaway from the photograph. He was fine, oh so fine and he kissed my hand.

But his family were not friendly, not at all! The parents looked me up and down and went silent. They drove me in a car to the house of a cousin. And I've been staying there on my own, waiting for Solomon to visit, waiting and waiting for the invitations to meet the nephews and nieces, the aunts and uncles, and for the rabbi to call. The cousin has been kind, telling me to be patient. Soon everything will be clear.

And now it is clear. Yesterday Solomon's mother came, with two of her sisters, all dressed in black. We sat in the parlour and she told me the decision. I am to go home. There will be no marriage. I am given no reasons.

'May they rot in hell,' says Bella's ma.

'May they shit blood and pus', says Bella's pa.

Sarah waits for the curses to subside, then continues. 'She cried and cried and begged to see Solomon but the mother refused. She said there was no point. He wasn't for her. She told Bella that they'd pay for the crossing and give her a small sum of money to cover her expenses.'

Sarah sifts the pages of the letter. ' Here,' she says, reading again:

His mother told me, 'Your parents will not be out of pocket. The next boat with a free berth sails in two weeks' time.' I cried, Sarah. How I cried. But yesterday evening there was a knock at the front door. It was Solomon. The cousin left us alone for a few minutes and he told me that he had begged for me to stay but his mother and father were determined. I must go. I asked him what I had done wrong and he told me I had done nothing. There were tears in his eyes. Then he shook my hand and hurried away.

So now I am writing this letter to you and I will hand it to the cousin and ask her to post it to you. I hope it reaches you before I do. Tell my parents that I did nothing wrong, that I have nothing to be ashamed of.

Your ever-loving friend Bella. ▌

Bella's ma weeps loudly.

'May all Pharoah's plagues be visited upon them,' she says.

'May leeches drink them dry,' says Pa.

***

By the time Bella returned, her parents had already received another visit, from Moishe the matchmaker this time, bringing a formal letter from the Schachat father, with a large banknote enclosed. Moishe was not known for his tact or taciturnity, so the full story of why Bella had been sent home was already out all over the village and Bella was the very last to hear. Ma and Pa came to the station to meet her. They put her trunk in the cart they had borrowed and snapped the reins. As the old horse trotted slowly back down the familiar tracks, they told her the truth. And it was just as well to let her know, before she heard it from the children playing in the dirt or the silly boys off to *shul*, with their smirks and their whispers.

'Bella's legs, Bella's legs,' they laughed. 'Bella's thighs, Bella's thighs,' they shouted in the *shul* yard, 'Bella's fella likes 'em thin,' but Bella had shut herself up in her room where she wouldn't have to hear.

'How could it be?' asked Sarah, a few weeks later, when Bella had finally decided to show her face again. 'They'd seen the photo, they'd said yes.'

'Ah,' said Bella. 'In their letter to Moishe they accused him of tricking them. The photographer from Plungė had schemed with him and my parents to show just my shoulders and face. I'd bewitched their son with the beauty of my face but my legs, they said, were as thick as tree trunks.'

Sarah shifted the little Plotkin over, to let him sleep more comfortably on the other side. 'But aren't you glad Bella, to be back home with us again and away from these strangers and their cruel behaviour? I always thought a Jew is a Jew and a *shtetl* Jew never changes his ways. It's deep down in his soul. But how wrong could I be? These Jews have travelled across the oceans to another world and they have forgotten who they are.'

'Yes,' said Bella. 'You're right,' she said but her voice was sad. 'He was so fine,' she said. 'Such a smile.' She wiped away a tear and then, 'But that's all done now and we won't ever mention it again.'

And that's what Bella planned. She was all ready to forget her long voyage out to a foreign land and her long voyage back again. She was glad to be back with her family for the Purim festival; she looked forward to collecting bilberries to make jam. There was work to be done helping her mother and she tried to put her mind to good things – a bar mitzvah, a dance, a trip to the river with her nieces and nephews, visits to the Plotkin home. She would remain in her parents' house and she would never marry. But perhaps she could live that life, without too many regrets.

Bella was settling back to life in the *shtetl*; the little boys had grown bored of their teasing and the taste of her bilberry jam and her home-made poppy-seed cakes made it hard to carry on laughing behind her back. She was Bella, the girl they'd known all their lives, after all. The one thing that she was touchy about was the subject of marriage. Ma had raised it a few times. There was a boy in a village nearby who was turning thirty, a nice boy not a *nebbish*. What did she think? She stormed off to her room and slammed the door.

One day, when she was washing sheets in the yard, pounding them hard in the bucket to make them white, she saw Moishe the Matchmaker walking down the road. A curse came to her lips but she held it back. It wasn't his fault after all. Instead of walking on past her house, he stopped and opened the gate.

'Good day to you Bella,' he said. 'Your ma it is with whom I wish to speak.'

She stood sullen and silent and pointed the way to the front door. She wanted to shout, 'No I won't marry the boy who's turning thirty from the village down the road and I won't marry any other *grober* or *schlemiel* that you've got on your books,' but she kept her mouth shut.

She hung the washing up to dry, then took herself off to the river, to sit by the bank and think. She lay down on the grass and stayed there like that for the rest of the afternoon. As the sun finally set below the trees, she picked herself up, dusted the grass from her skirts and trudged back to her house on the other side of the village.

Ma and Pa were sitting in the kitchen waiting for her, their faces pale with worry. 'There's been a letter,' said Pa straightaway. 'They want you back.'

Bella sat on the bottom step and put her head in her hands.

'It's the boy,' Ma said. 'He isn't happy. He's told them he wants you back. It's you he wants to marry.'

'He's pining, they say. He's losing weight. They're worried about their boy.'

Bella didn't look up.

'Of course, we said no straightaway,' said Pa. 'You're not just a parcel to be sent backwards and forwards, a piece of freight. A flat rejection we gave. So that's that.'

Bella looked up. 'The boy, you say?' she said. 'It's the boy who wants me back?'

'A three-week journey across the world and back again and they have the *chutzpah* to ask you to return? They must be *meshugeneh*, mad people! Are their heads in their *tokheses*?'

'I'm going,' she said. 'When's the next sailing from Libau?'

And that's how Bella became my great-aunt. She climbed onto a cart in the marketplace at Gargzdai that took her to the station, from where she took the steam train to Libau and crossed the oceans in a slightly more expensive cabin (negotiated by Moishe) and walked down the gangplank at Cape Town once again, to be greeted by Solomon Schachat, who bowed down and kissed her hand.

After the wedding, a small ceremony with just the family, she settled in a house in Vredehoek. My great-uncle Solly devoted himself to her. They had three children and they were happy. When she talked to the children of her life in the *shtetl* and her journey to Cape Town, there was only one voyage, no more. And they were glad, for they knew that her travels across the oceans had given them life and had carried her away from a world where her ma and pa, her brothers and sisters, her friend Sarah Plotkin and all the little Plotkins would have their houses and haystacks burned and their blood spilled in the snow.

THE THIRD-FLOOR BEDROOM

KATE DICAMILLO

> **Kate DiCamillo** (1964-) is an American who writes for both children and adults. 'The Third-floor Bedroom' was first published in *The Chronicles of Harris Burdick* in 2011. This is a collection of stories by well-known authors responding to another book, called *The Mysteries of Harris Burdick.*
>
> This book consists of a series of very detailed images by the American author and illustrator Chris Van Allsburg. Each image has a caption. The image DiCamillo used as inspiration is included on page 154. The caption to the image is, 'It all began when someone left the window open.'

MARCH 28, 1944

Dear Martin,

I am a prisoner. Did you know that this would happen when you put me on the train to her? She has very fat ankles, Martin. You insist that she is our aunt, but I don't believe that it's possible for me to be related to someone with such fat ankles. And I'm not lying: I am a prisoner! She locks me in this room. She has a key that she keeps in her apron and she uses it to lock the door behind her; and after the door is locked, she rattles the doorknob, checking herself. I can feel the rattling of that doorknob in my teeth. I have extremely sensitive teeth. I don't know if you remember this about me. Sometimes I worry that you won't remember me at all.

'It all began when someone left the window open.'

In any case you might like to know that the room (my prison!) is on the third floor. I can see mountains. There is some consolation in that (the seeing the mountains), but not enough that you should think l feel cheerful. I don't. I feel abandoned. In fact, my feelings of abandonment are at this very moment so profoundly overwhelming that I am forced to bring this letter to a close. Mrs Bullwhyte taught us that all good letters should end with a summation, followed by an offering of good wishes. Here is my summation: I am a prisoner. The 'relative' who is keeping me prisoner has fat ankles. Also, I didn't mention it earlier, but I am sick. Here are my good wishes for you: I hope you don't get shot.

Cordially your sister,

Pearlie George Lamott

P.S. What do they feed you in the army? Who feeds you? I am a good cook. I could have taken care of myself while you were away.

P.P.S. I didn't bat an eye when Ma left, did I? I expected it, Martin. But I did not ever expect that you would leave me. ∎

MARCH 29, 1944

Dear Martin,

Here is a sketch of the wallpaper in my prison. As you can see, there is a bird and then another bird and then another bird and then another bird. There is a vine and then another vine and then another vine and then another vine (although it could all be the same vine; it's impossible to tell for certain and I've given up trying). There is a word for this wallpaper and that word (one of Mrs Bullwhyte's vocabulary words, which she would be happy to see me make proper use of) is relentless. The wallpaper is so relentless that when I close my eyes against it, I still see it. Even if I weren't locked in this room, I would feel as if I were imprisoned here due to the relentlessness of the wallpaper. It's as if the whole room is under the spell of some witch (a witch with fat ankles). Do you know that once Mrs. Bullwhyte said about me (in front of the whole class) that she has never known a child with such a propensity for verbiage? It pleased me inordinately when she said that. But I must tell you that since I have arrived here, I have not spoken one word. Not one, Martin. Bringing this letter to a close, I will say, in summation, that I am caught in the lair of a witch. My good wishes to you (the recipient of this letter) are that I continue to hope you don't get shot.

Your sister,

Pearlie George Lamott

P.S. You should know that I am very sick. This happened when I set out to try to find you. I was outside for one full night and it was very rainy and I slept in the crook of a tree and I caught a cold. (Mrs Bullwhyte said that it is a superstition, an old wives' tale, that you can catch cold from merely being cold. I am sorry to disappoint her, but that is what happened to me.) I didn't believe when I set out to find you that I would actually find you. But I felt duty-bound to look. I want to be clear. (Mrs Bullwhyte said that we should always strive for clarity of language, as it is a gift to our reader.) So here I am, being clear, Martin: I wasn't running away, I was running toward.

P.P.S. I wonder if those wallpaper birds feel as trapped as I do. It's hard for me to breathe in here.

MARCH 30, 1944

Dear Martin,

Today the doctor came. Don't ask me his name. I can't remember it; but I think it begins with an F. All I can tell you for certain is that he is a nose whistler. Various and assorted tunes came out of his nose as he examined me. At one point, he got through most of 'Begin the Beguine', although I'm not sure he intended a tune at all. He does not, by nature, seem like the kind of man who likes a song. Dour is the Bullwhyte vocabulary word that could be properly used to describe him. He listened for a long time to my lungs, but I don't know how he could have heard anything at all over the whistling of his own nose. In any case, I believe that he is looking in the wrong place, as whatever is wrong with me has nothing at all to do with my lungs. The only good that came of his visit is that he said I must have fresh air, and so the window in my room has been opened. Mrs. Bullwhyte once read us a story that started with the words 'It all began when someone left the window open.' I can't remember a thing that happened in that story. But I've been singing those words to myself now like a song, 'It all began, it all began, it all began when someone left window open.' I have never smelled air so sweet, Martin. I could, I would fly away. Not toward. Away.

Your sister,

Pearlie

P.S. Instead of a summation, I'm offering this interesting piece of information. I guess it is best that you hear it from me (as opposed to hearing it from 'Aunt' Hazel). I bit the doctor. It surprised everyone. It surprised even me. He provoked me. He accused me of being feral. 'Has she been raised by wolves?' he said when I refused to answer his questions. She (the fat-ankled 'Aunt' Hazel) tried to defend me. She said that I was, for all intents and purposes, an orphan. The doctor said that that was absolutely no excuse, and that at twelve years of age I was almost grown and should act like an adult and speak when spoken to.

In any case, that is neither here nor there (as Mrs. Bullwhyte said to me often enough when I rambled on attempting to explain something that turned out not to be explainable at all). What matters is that I thought I would live up to the doctor's expectations of me and act as if I were raised by wolves, and so I bit him. It was only a small bite, not really wolf-like at all. I didn't even break the skin. Or, I do not think I did.

P.P.S. Here are my good wishes for you: you can, if you want, describe what it is like to be in the army. I will listen to you. I have always listened to you.

THE END OF MARCH, 1944

Dear Martin,

Today a big crow came and sat on the windowsill and looked right directly at me. He stared at me so long that I believe he was working to memorise my face. I would like to think that he then flew out of here, over the mountains and over the sea and right directly to you, holding the whole time this picture of me in his dark head and that when he landed beside you, you looked into his eyes and saw *me*; and that you could see how angry I am and how sick I am and how positively full and brimming-to-burst with words I am. This is what Mrs. Bullwhyte would call one of my 'extended flights of fancy'. She said that I am terribly prone to them and often told me that I should rein myself in or the world was bound to disappoint me. And guess what, Martin? She was right. The world has disappointed me. You let yourself get drafted; you have gone off to war, I am alone in the world. In summation: the mountains outside my window look purple sometimes, and sometimes they look blue. The mountains are always offered up in poetry and the Bible as something solid and true, but my thought on that is this: how could anyone trust in something so changeable, blue one minute and purple the next? My wishes for you: last night, the moon was very low in the sky. It gave off a strange light that that made the wallpaper birds seem to flap their wings. Take that and turn it into a wish for yourself, Martin.

Your sister,

Pearlie

P.S. When you walked away from me at the train station, I watched you for as long as I was able, as long as was humanly possible, and you did not look back, not once. That is when my heart broke. What's wrong with me has nothing to do with my lungs. That nose-whistling, F-named doctor doesn't know what he's doing. It's my heart, my heart. My heart.

I'M NOT SURE WHEN IT IS

Martin,

I have pneumonia and a high fever and it is hard for me to write these words. Everything shimmers; nothing holds still. I hope you appreciate my effort to communicate, Martin. *It is our duty and our joy to communicate our hearts to each other. Words assist us in this task.* That is what was written at the top of every one of Mrs Bullwhyte's vocabulary lists. Aunt Hazel sits with me and cries a lot and communicates with me that way. I have taken pity on her and allowed her to move her chair close to my bed. She is right beside me. In between crying she talks and tells me astonishing things. For one: our mother was always flighty, even when she was a child (I guess this isn't that astonishing). And that if she (Aunt Hazel) had known that we had been left all alone (she never even knew that Pa had died), she would not have allowed it. She would have come for us. I can't imagine someone coming for us. I'd like to think about it more, but I can't. I can't think about anything right now. I'm so hot. The air coming in the window smells like mountains and the black wings of crows. If I could say something to Aunt Hazel, if I could manage to make myself speak, I would say that I'm not mad anymore, only afraid, and I don't want to leave the world.

Pearlie

APRIL 8, 1944

Dear Martin,

Aunt Hazel and I were together in the third floor bedroom for an eternity. This, of course, is hyperbole. But hyperbole is sometimes necessary to get at the truth (it seems odd doesn't it, that we have to lie to tell the truth better?). But that is neither here nor there. What I mean to say is that I was feverish for a long time and that Aunt Hazel stayed with me for the whole of it. That is a fact. It is also a fact that Aunt Hazel begged me to speak. Begged me, Martin. I have never before in my life had anyone beg for me to speak. It was deeply satisfying particularly because for most of my life, I have been encouraged (vehemently) to keep quiet.

In any case, what happened was that I was in the grips of the fever, and

I had a movie running in my head and what I kept seeing were not old, sad images, the kind you would expect your brain to pull up when you are sick and maybe dying; images such as Pa's funeral, how black everything (the coffin and the trees and his hair, all slicked back) was and the way you sat on a chair in the dining room afterward and put your head in your hands like an old man; or an image of the house the way it looked (curtains blowing and the light forlorn) the morning I woke up and knew that Ma was well and truly gone; or the sight of you, walking away at the train station, never once turning back. I saw none of that. What I saw instead the whole time the fever raged was a moving list of Mrs Bullwhyte's vocabulary words. Every word looked as if it were etched in fire, necessary and demanding. I couldn't help but think that Mrs Bullwhyte would be pleased about this. At some point, I started to say the words out loud. Aunt Hazel listened to me with her mouth hanging open, as if I were speaking words she had been waiting all her life to hear. I have never been listened to that way. It's an absolute shame that what I said didn't make any sense. I just said the words, read them from the list, and when I finally stopped, I felt freer, lighter, as if I might float away. Aunt Hazel, seeing this, took hold of my hand.

And then, as I was looking straight ahead, staring at nothing but the wall, an amazing thing happened. One of the birds broke free. It unpeeled itself from the wallpaper and flew around the room, bright as light, and then it went out of the open window. Another bird lifted its wing off the wall and Aunt Hazel squeezed my hand so hard that it hurt, and after a minute, the bird sighed and sank back into the wall and stayed.

You will say that this was fever and Mrs Bullwhyte would say that it was an extended flight of fancy, but I can only tell you that it is true: what was nothing but paper transformed itself into something living right before my eyes. I fell asleep then, and when I woke up it was dark in the room and Aunt Hazel was still there by my bed, sleeping and holding on to my hand. Can you imagine that? I've come to believe that her thick ankles are a clue to her character. Stalwart. That is the Bullwhyte vocabulary word for Aunt Hazel. The door to my room was unlocked. I took my hand out of Aunt Hazel's and got out of bed and went to the door and opened it all the way and stepped down the hallway and down the stairs and into the kitchen and made myself a sandwich of cheese and bread. The bread was stale, but I have never in my life tasted such a good piece of cheese. I thought about

Aunt Hazel, upstairs, asleep in her chair. She has very large hands, Martin, and she had held on to me so tight. And then I remembered the wallpaper bird, breaking free and flying out the window. My legs got shaky and I had to sit down. I sat there in the kitchen and held my sandwich; and I believed suddenly, fiercely, that I was going to live and so were you. I could feel the promise of this, of our surviving, deep in the enamel of my highly sensitive teeth. I finished the sandwich and went back upstairs and Aunt Hazel was still there, sleeping by my bed, and I said her name again and again until she finally woke up.

Your sister,

Pearlie

P.S. In summation: I am almost entirely well. Aunt Hazel is stalwart. It is April now, at last.

P.P.S. My wishes for you: that when you come home, you will go upstairs with me, to the third floor bedroom, and let me show you the break in the pattern of the wallpaper, the place where a bird was and should be and is not. This is proof of something I am sure, although I cannot say exactly what. When you turn away from the wallpaper, I will direct your gaze to the mountains, which are waiting, still, outside my window. As I write these words to you, they are changing again. They are turning themselves green.